What People Are Saying About the *7F Words*™

"This book is 'fantastic'...It sucked me in right away... I wanted to read more and learn more about how I too can manage my time better and have more fun in life... It has inspired me to set new goals and to get my business and life on track. I believe that often times we get into a 'rut' and allow ourselves to just go day-to-day. We are not unhappy, but we just don't have the 'it' factor. With all the *7F Words*™ put into practice it helps us to become the better 'me'..."

Bonnie Adams
Diversified Distributors

"This is just what the doctor ordered. Except the prescription is easy to read and understand. A wonderful reference book to keep coming back to. Thank you for sharing your hearts and minds. Your spirits shine through."

Karon Clark
2013 President Women's Council of REALTORS®
Greater Palm Beach County Chapter

"Looking back at my life events I realized that, without knowing how or why, I had applied all of the *7F Words*™ without benefit of a book. Now retired, it is easy to look back on my careers and see how the *7F Words*™ applied. I said careers because I ran multiple businesses, with 100+ employees, and the self-required 100+ hour work week. My only shortfall was to balance all of them consistently. I would encourage using this tool to achieve not only balance but also be successful and happy on your path to retirement."

Daniel B. Durbin
Retired and loving it

"What a wonderful guide to the fundamentals of life's journey with a focus on balance. It provides a lifelong road map for action, encouragement and staying on track. An easy read that will continue as a reference for years to come. Enjoy reading and putting into action. A masterpiece by Barbara, Deborah and Cathy!"

Sue Flaig
Past National President, Women's Council of REALTORS®

"Cathy, Barbara and Deborah have done a masterful job of showing us how to simplify and integrate the seven distinct elements of our day-to-day existence into living a balanced life. A 'must-read' for anyone seeking that sweet equilibrium."

Donna Greenspan-Solomon, Esq.
Solomon Appeals, Mediation & Arbitration

"It is Fantastic that the Certified Sisters put this Fascinating book together with just *7F Words*™! I am confident that the impact on its readers will be Forever!! Happy Birthday and keep the good work going!!!"

Dr. Charles Lee

"I consider this book a must-have for anyone wanting to live a happier more fulfilled life. What are the dreams you hold for yourself? This book is a beautiful instruction guide to achieve a life of freedom and happiness. I have read many books promising joy in my life, yet I have read none as simple and practical as the *7F Words*™."

Sharon Loyd
Aviation Source

"Do yourself a favor and read this book now! The authors of this book know what it takes to set you on the path of a balanced life. Fortunately for us, they share it with clarity of concept and presentation!"

Veronica L. McManus 2013 President MA State Chapter
Women's Council of REALTORS®

"*7F Words*™ so simple -- yet so brilliant. We recognize these words individually each day; yet together they bring an inspiring and powerful message. These authentic and heartfelt stories will gently challenge the reader into action. This book is a compass to living the life God intended for each of us. Well done Ladies, I look forward to passing it along!"

Holly Robillard
SAHM(Stay at Home Mom) and Entrepreneur

"... Please, read the book. It's not long or complicated... I truly believe that anyone who does so and starts to make and check off their own list, will soon find that the *7F Words*™ is a very effective way to maintain balance and harmony with your own life. It challenges you by making sure you challenge yourself..."

Brian Rothschild
GraphicFXOnline

"It's an easy to remember-and-do concept for happiness and success that is simple and basic and basically brilliant."

Julia Sansevere
Coldwell Banker Residential Real Estate

"Where we are today in each area of our lives is truly our 'minimum standard'. To grow and enrich our lives, planning needs to be done to push ourselves to where we want to be; to reach our goals. The *7F Words*™ has been superbly written to advance you on your journey. Congratulations Barbara, Deborah and Cathy for writing a must read book!"

Angela Territo
Training & Coaching, LLC.

Date:

To:

From:

Power Strategies to Transform Your Life

Barbara D. Agerton
Deborah A. Bacarella
Catherine A. Lewis

Certified Sisters™, Inc.

7F Words™ For Living a Balanced Life

Copyright © 2013 by Certified Sisters™, Inc.,
Barbara D. Agerton, Deborah A. Bacarella
and Catherine A. Lewis

Printed in the United States of America
ISBN-10: 0989976807
ISBN-13: 978-0989976800

To purchase copies go to www.amazon.com.

Make every day a "7" at: www.7FWords.com.

The following oath is a daily reminder to touch on each of the *7F Words*™. Say it every day and you'll see how quickly you begin to make these elements a priority in your life.

7F WORDS™ DAILY OATH

Today I will <u>Focus</u> on improving the balance in my life.

I will have <u>Faith</u> in my ability to succeed in all I do.

I will allow myself the <u>Freedom</u> to say no to things I do not want to do or that will not advance me toward my goals.

I will spend time nurturing my relationships with my <u>Family</u> and those who are important to me.

I will be conscious of my <u>Finances</u> and act accordingly.

I will take action to ensure my mental and physical <u>Fitness</u>.

And, last but not least, today I will have <u>Fun</u>.

Go to www.7FWords.com to download the *7F Words*™ Oath template so you can create your own daily oath.

Certified Sisters™, *Inc. endeavors to empower individuals to transform their lives by providing a framework and power strategies to plan and intentionally live each day with joy and purpose.*

This book is dedicated to hard-working women and men everywhere who are searching for a better plan to live life with purpose and intent.

Contents

Foreword by Maurice "Moe" Veissi,   x

    National Association of REALTORS® 2012 President

How the Seed Was Planted   xi

Acknowledgements   xiv

About The Logo   xvi

Inspiration for the 7F Words™ Colors   xvii

Chapter 1: *Focus* – Laser Beam Focus   1

Chapter 2: *Faith* – Taking the First Step,   19

    What I Learned From a Squirrel

Chapter 3: *Freedom* –Ruthlessly Prioritize and   39

    Learn to Say No

Chapter 4: *Family* – How to Create Balance   49

    With the Most Important People in Your Life

Chapter 5: *Finance* – Put The Plug In,   59

    Or It All Goes Down the Drain

Chapter 6: *Fitness* – How to Put Some   73

    Panache In Your Life

Chapter 7: *Fun* – Find the Fun, Forget the Stress   93

Transformation Stories   106

About the Authors   117

References   119

7F Words™

Foreword

The level of an individual's engagement in any relationship be it spousal, friendships, business related, social, spiritual, or a myriad of others, is always predicated on the weakest commitment between the interacting individuals. We tend to consider the lowest bar set as the acceptable measure of satisfaction. It's not a good thing or bad thing; it's the way we humans most often respond to our associations. Wouldn't it be nice if we all could wake up each morning to a set of metrics created solely to raise our spirits and the level of the bar we want to achieve? Well, here is the answer. You have it in your hands right now! The *7F Words*™ can launch you on a lifetime journey by following a simple, life-altering course that will make the bar you set fun, extremely achievable and enormously productive.

The *7F Words*™ offers a simple formula for life-improving relationships, business excellence, and a self-enhancing blueprint aimed at living and appreciating your life to its fullest. Give yourself a gift each day and incorporate the *7F Words*™ into your daily routine, your bar will ever be set higher, and you will always know that the life you live is infinitely more important than anything else you can offer this world.

Maurice "Moe" Veissi
National Association of REALTORS® 2012 President

How the Seed Was Planted

Deborah

The seed for the *7F Words*™ was planted one spectacular, sunny South Florida afternoon when I was having lunch with my customer, Dr. Lee at one of Boca Raton's finest country clubs. The food was delicious, the service outstanding and the lush tropical landscape outside our window was nothing short of paradise. Anyone who happened to look my way would have thought I was having the time of my life, until one simple question from Dr. Lee caused me to burst into tears.

"When was the last time you had fun?"

This occurred shortly after the real estate bubble in Florida had burst. My husband and I were real estate professionals, trying to maintain an office and support our family. Like most people in the sales industry we were working twice as hard for less than half the money. The real estate horizon was very grim at the time and as a mother, wife and business owner I was pulled in so many directions that there was nothing left at the end of the day. "Fun" was a foreign word.

Dr. Lee's question made me face the fear, exhaustion and frustration I had been experiencing and I finally admitted something had to change. I realized that my life was out of balance, work was encroaching on every aspect of my existence.

My faith was wavering, my children missed me, my bank account was dwindling and I was neglecting my physical and mental health. My life was out of control. I was definitely not having fun!

That night, still shaken and embarrassed from my emotional breakdown in front of Dr. Lee, I had divine inspiration as I slept. When I woke up I immediately grabbed a pen so I could write it all down. I made a list of the things that were the most important in my life. I wrote out the seven "F" words that would change my life forever and then promptly put them into my "Dream Folder" where I neglected them for two years while I kept on trying to "work it out." During those two years, amid the real estate collapse, both Cathy Lewis and I, as real estate sales professionals, found we were putting our customers' needs ahead of our family and our health. We were in constant fear of losing the next potential sale, so we sacrificed our lives in pursuit of the next deal.

We witnessed the same phenomenon in people around us not just real estate agents, but people in all walks of life: teachers, bankers, insurance agents, and anyone from small business owners to corporate executives. It seemed that just about everyone was struggling to earn a living while at the same time finding it extremely difficult to balance all the other important aspects of their lives.

Cathy and I had talked about co-authoring a book to help REALTORS®. When we actually sat down to begin mapping out the book, I pulled out my "Dream Folder" of potential book titles that I had been keeping since before my encounter with Dr. Lee. The 7 F words jumped out at us. Cathy said "That's it!" Right then, we decided to write a book that would help us, as well as others, focus on the important aspects of life while still earning a living.

The *7F Words*™ we identified as the most important elements of a productive, healthy and happy life are Focus, Faith, Freedom, Family, Finance, Fitness and Fun. Realizing that Finance was one of the critical "F" Words we asked my sister Barbara, a Certified Public Accountant, to collaborate with us on the book.

It has been an incredible journey. We've shared some laughs, a few tears and some great stories that will inspire you just as they did us. After reading the *7F Words*™ we are convinced that you will come away with a new set of Power Strategies and attitudes to help you balance your daily demands and lead a more fulfilled and joyful life.

So join me and my Certified Sisters™ on this journey through the *7F Words*™ *for Living a Balanced Life*! And by the way, writing this book and presenting the workshops has been a lot of FUN!

ACKNOWLEDGMENTS

Thanks to Deborah and Cathy. You motivate me every day. Our weekly Skype calls have become somewhat of a therapy session. I've learned more about my sister and what an incredible person she is. And I've gained a new *"Certified Sister*™*"* in Cathy. You both are so creative, throwing ideas at me like the ball machine in a batting cage. The ideas bounce around me and I want to catch them all. So we've caught some of the ideas here. I hope you get as much from your daily *7F Words*™ as I have.

Barbara

I thank God for the divine vision of the *7F Words*™ that inspired this book. Thank you to my family, friends and customers who have shared their stories with me. My hope is that these *7F Words*™ will motivate you to make positive changes in your life and enable you to live your dreams. Pay it forward by passing along the *7F Words*™ to encourage others to implement positive changes in their lives. And most of all remember to have Fun! Enjoy the journey!

Deborah

Deborah and Barbara, the two of you have had such a positive impact on my life. This book is just the beginning of our journey and already the rewards have been many. You inspire me and keep me moving toward our vision for Certified Sisters™, Inc. I envision an organization that will empower women to help others throughout the world. I want to express my heartfelt thanks to my husband, Jim, who always believes in me and supports my efforts. And, to all my other special friends and family who share my joy, lend their ears and calm my fears, I love you all.

Cathy

Many thanks to those who helped us prepare this book for publishing. Julia Sansevere, Charlene Smith, Michele Bacarella, Michael Bacarella, Karon Clark, Sherry Weissman, Sharon Loyd, Jim Lewis and Evelyn Lewis generously gave their time and expertise in editing. Thanks to Brian Rothschild for creating our wonderful book cover and prepress guidance, to LuAnn Warner-Prokos, photographer for our beautiful cover photograph and to Harry Lee Chester, Jr. for the soaring eagle photograph in the Freedom chapter. Thank you Tom Gnadinger Photography for the family photo. We are grateful to Pastor J.R. Jones for his squirrel story, Jennifer Kuhlman for F2 and F3 Family Fun, Dale Manno for her advice on freedom from clutter and Christine King for her inspirational story of physical fitness and recovery. And for all the others who motivate us to make every day a 7!

About The Logo

Our graphic artist, Kaizen Creative from 99 Designs created this beautiful logo. He put a lot of thought into the design. The shape of the bird provides a stylized image of the "7F" and brings together all the words in a delicate, meaningful and colorful form.

FOCUS is symbolized by the EYE. Focus is about keeping your eye on the goal.

FAITH is symbolized by the HEAD. Faith is the best guide to direct your life.

FREEDOM is symbolized by the WING. Freedom can take you anywhere you wish to go.

FAMILY is symbolized by the HEART. Family are those you love and keep close to your heart.

FINANCE is symbolized by the MOUTH. Finances are essential to feed yourself and your family.

FITNESS is symbolized by the BODY. Fitness keeps your body and mind healthy.

FUN is symbolized by the BACK & TAIL. Fun allows you to sit back and enjoy life. The tail also functions to maintain balance in flight. Fun brings balance to your life and makes life itself worth living.

Inspiration for the *7F Words*™ Colors

The colors associated with each of our *7F Words*™ were inspired by Judy Scott-Kemmis, the creator of the Empower Yourself With Color Psychology website. She is a color consultant who studied color and design at the School of Colour and Design in Sydney, Australia. Our colors were chosen from some of the positive keywords she associates with the respective colors.

FOCUS – RED: action, speed, attention, assertiveness, confidence, energy, stimulation, excitement, power, passion, drive, strength, courage and determination.

FAITH – MAGENTA: universal harmony and love, emotional balance, spiritual yet practical, loving, compassionate, supportive and kind.

FREEDOM – ORANGE: sociable, optimistic, enthusiastic, cheerful, self-confident, independent, flamboyant, extroverted and uninhibited, adventurous, risk-taker, creative flair, warm-hearted, agreeable and informal.

FAMILY – BLUE: loyalty, trust and integrity, reliability and responsibility, caring and concern, devotion, peaceful and calm.

FINANCE – GREEN: growth and vitality, renewal and restoration, self-reliance, reliability and dependability, emotionally balanced and calm, nature lover and family oriented, practical and generous.

FITNESS – TURQUOISE: communication, clarity of thought, balance and harmony, idealism, calmness, creativity, compassion, healing and self-sufficiency.

FUN – YELLOW: optimism, cheerfulness, enthusiasm, good-humor, confidence, originality, creativity and challenge.

*Today I will **Focus** on improving the balance in my life.*

Focus: a state or condition permitting clear perception or understanding

Merriam-Webster

Chapter 1

Focus

Then the LORD replied: "Write down the revelation and make it plain on tablets so that a herald may run with it." Habakkuk 2:2

Why is it that most of us are reluctant to commit our goals to paper? Why is it that we make New Year's resolutions only to lose sight of them before the end of January? Is it something in our DNA? Is it fear of failure? Is it fear of success? Maybe it's just too difficult or perhaps it's just not fun. More likely than not we don't fully commit because we don't really see what's in it for us.

It's very easy to let life get in the way of doing what needs to be done to achieve our goals. Often we don't even know what it is we want to achieve. We go from day to day reacting to things that are thrown in our way, so it's very easy to lose sight of our priorities. Are you living your life like a ship without a rudder, aimlessly bobbing around and never reaching your destination? Wouldn't it be great to be standing at the helm of your ship, with the wind in your hair, knowing that you are going full speed ahead and confident that you are going to reach your destination?

To live the most positive and balanced life, we need to understand what makes us feel happy and fulfilled. Then we need to move forward with intent to build happiness and fulfillment into our lives through accomplishing our goals.

Some of the greatest achievers are those who have mastered the art of laser beam focus. They know exactly what they want and are always focused on the target. Every action they take brings them closer to achieving their goals.

To achieve a goal, we must first be able to see it clearly in our mind and then make a firm commitment to make it happen. We must be able to visualize the positive outcome it will have on us. All of our senses must be engaged.

Vision Statement

Cathy

One of the most powerful and poignant exercises Deborah and I do as Professional Coaches is to create a vision statement for our clients. The vision statement allows us to provide the client with a clear picture of what their life could look like in some specifically defined time in the future. We create the vision statement after asking pertinent questions and listening to what the client tells us is their dream for the future. We read the vision statement to the client when they are in a relaxed state and can focus on the vision without distraction. In that relaxed state they can almost feel, taste, hear, smell and see what is being described to them.

Below is the vision statement I wrote for Deborah.

"Deborah, close your eyes and relax. Take a deep breath and then gently exhale, sending a wave of relaxation from the top of your head to the tips of your toes. A sense of peace and warmth encompasses your entire being. You are totally without stress and worry.

Now envision a beautiful, sunny South Florida morning. You are sitting on the back patio of your new oceanfront home in Boca Raton. Fragrant tropical flowers and lush green plants surround you. The smell of the ocean wafts in on a light breeze and you can hear the sounds of the surf and the cries of the seagulls above.

You feel completely energized as you have just finished the morning strength training workout that your personal trainer designed for you. You are at your optimal weight and are proud of the fact that you have achieved much improved health through exercise and healthy eating. As a matter of fact, your loving husband Michael has just brought you a wonderful breakfast of healthy oatmeal with fresh bananas and mangoes that he grew in the garden, along with a cup of fragrant herbal tea.

As you sip your tea you marvel at the grace that God has bestowed on you. You have achieved your highest career goals and can now live humbly, without financial concerns, on only ten percent of your income. And you were able to give the remaining ninety percent to charities and organizations that bring peace and love to the world. You are truly going to leave an important legacy. You have given God the glory in all that you accomplished. You are delighted to spend meaningful time in attending and leading bible study and prayer groups.

As you take in all the magnificent sights and sounds around you, you reminisce on the family reunion you and Michael attended last month in Kentucky. Michael Anthony, Marissa and Michele were all there with their significant others. It was such a gift that all seven of your brothers and sisters were able to make it along with many of their family members. You pick up and reread the beautiful card signed by all three children expressing their gratitude for the fun vacation that you gave them. They are now each successful in their own right and you reflect on how proud you are of the young adults they turned out to be.

Just now you hear the phone ring and it is a call from Adam, your top producer at Elite Florida Real Estate. Only four years ago he started as your intern, right out of college with a marketing degree. You took him under your wing and mentored him in all the important aspects of real estate. He is now earning a six figure income.

No sooner do you hang up with Adam than you get a call from Cathy, one of your co-authors of the *7F Words*™ *for Living a Balanced Life* and co-founder of Certified Sisters™, Inc. Cathy is calling to tell you that she picked up the tickets for the gala event that you will be attending this evening. At the event, you, Cathy and your sister and third co-author, Barbara, will be receiving a humanitarian award for your work in helping others to lead balanced and productive lives.

Before you leave your patio for a walk on the beach you take a minute to thank the Lord for the peace and contentment you now enjoy. You are not only debt free, but you are able to give back in a very significant way. You have accomplished your goal of leaving a legacy, your children are flourishing and the two businesses you have built are making money for you while you sleep. Life is GOOD."

• • • • • • •

For help with creating your own vision statement, go to www.7FWords.com and download your free questionnaire.

Vision Board

A vision board takes the Vision Statement one step further. It helps you depict what you want to achieve or have in your life. It helps you envision and stay focused on your goals.

You can create a vision board using various mediums such as a poster or a cork board with pictures from magazines, brochures and cut out words or phrases. Or, you can go high-tech and use an online computer program or app.

Based on the Vision Statement I created for Deborah, her Vision Board might contain pictures of the following:

- A lush garden with tropical trees laden with succulent fruit
- A magnificent house on the beach
- A snapshot of someone giving a speech in a huge auditorium
- Someone receiving an award
- The words "Certified Sisters" or "Elite Florida Real Estate" on the marquee of a stately office building
- Someone running along the beach
- An invitation to a family reunion
- A picture of a sumptuous healthy meal with the recipe below it
- A wheelbarrow full of money

Realistically speaking, the act of putting these wonderful things on a vision board is not going make them magically happen. Deborah would have to continue to focus on those goals every day, prioritize them and take positive action to accomplish them.

A vision board is an effective daily reminder to keep your eye on the ball. If you want to hit the home run you have to step up to the plate and swing the bat with power and precision. To make the most of a vision board you need to add the action steps like we did by adding the recipe below the picture of the healthy meal.

In his video *The Power of Vision,* Joel Barker says "Vision without action is merely a dream. Action without vision just passes the time. Vision with action can change the world."

SMART Goals
Cathy

Earlier I suggested that one reason we don't stick to our goals is that it's just not fun. What if it could be fun to set and achieve goals? How would it feel to be able to check off your accomplishments every day and know that you've come closer to the success you deserve?

As professional life coaches we help our clients write SMART goals. SMART is an easy memory aid for including the key elements of an effective goal statement.

S for Specific

M for Measurable

A for Attainable

R for Relevant

T for Time-bound

So, why not start with a goal to do something fun that will give you a sense of joy and build a lifelong memory? It could look something like this: "I will go to a Broadway play with my best friend before the end of this year." This goal is specific because it states a definite action you're going to take. It's measurable because you'll achieve a material or quantifiable outcome. The fact that it's something within your control makes it attainable. It's relevant because it pertains to something you want to do and time-bound as there is a specific end date.

Now you try it. Think of something that you would like to do that will give you a great deal of pleasure. Ask yourself if it's realistic. Determine the best way to measure it and set a deadline for completion. Take out a piece of paper and pen, use your computer or tablet, but whatever the medium, the important thing is to commit your goal to writing. Now, visualize yourself actually doing what you've written down. Can you see it in your mind? How does it feel? Can you almost experience a true sense of enjoyment?

Once you've finished writing your goal statement you need to determine your action steps to accomplish the goal. If you're going to a Broadway show you'll need to:

- Identify the show you'd like to see
- Determine when and where it's playing
- Compare calendars with your friend and choose a day
- Plan the trip
- Estimate the cost and set aside the funds
- Purchase the tickets
- Arrange for work coverage, and/or child or pet care

So, you can see that just one goal has many steps you need to focus on in order to make the goal a reality and there must be a logical sequence of events.

What if you purchased the ticket but neglected to arrange the date ahead of time with your friend or didn't check availability of transportation? You would not be able to achieve the goal. What could get in the way of accomplishing this goal? You need certain resources like time or money. How can you get the resources you need? Surely if this is a realistic goal there are many ways you can attain what you need. Get creative, think outside the box as they say. For example, if the ticket price is over your budget you might

9

consider being flexible and going to a matinee that might be less expensive or try to get discounted tickets. Or, instead of going to New York City to see a Broadway show you could find a show you'd like to see in a nearby city. You might use this as an opportunity to clean out your closet and bring those items that you're not using to a consignment shop. Put the money you get from selling those unused items toward your show ticket.

No matter what your goal, you will have a much greater chance of accomplishing it if you can: see the value in it, visualize the outcome in great detail, assign a time for completion, and measure the success.

Mapping
Barbara

When I was young I decided I wanted to be a Certified Public Accountant. That was my goal. I realize something now that at the time did not occur to me. I had a goal; it was specific, measurable, attainable, relevant, and time-bound. All the action steps were already mapped out for me. As an accounting student I was given a course guide and told what courses to take and when so I could earn my degree. Mapping was the part that I would never have been able to do on my own.

How do you map out the action steps needed to reach your goal? Let's look at some mapping tools and techniques that have helped some of my business clients.

First, you don't need to reinvent the wheel. Look for others who have already accomplished what you're trying to do and do what they did. When I was a kid we played "copycat" to the utter annoyance of my older brothers and sisters. It was a great way for me as the youngest to emulate their behavior. Since I had awesome brothers and sisters, I learned a lot of good stuff. Use the copycat technique for accomplishing your goals.

The best example of the copycat technique that I've seen is the franchise model. Think about the last time you drove somewhere. Did you see a McDonald's or a Starbucks along the way? Most likely you did. One of the reasons the franchise model is so successful is because they have made all the stores the same. The way the store opens in the morning, the food they serve, how the food is prepared, how they keep the books and on and on. When you buy a franchise you are effectively purchasing a map of how to create a successful business. That takes us right back to mapping which I think is key to accomplishing anything worthwhile. Keep in mind you don't need to purchase a franchise to mimic their map. Study the business or the person that is doing what you want to do and then learn from them.

Tools, we all like tools. That's just a fact of life, whether it is a hammer or a drill, or a laptop or smart phone. The goal mapping tool that I like is a computer program called Mind Map by Mindjet.com. They have some wonderful templates to get you started, such as project management maps, personal dashboard maps and event planning maps. Think about mapping your goals the same as planning a car trip. In the old days you would get out the Road Atlas and turn to the states you would be crossing and highlight the route. Then you would get the ruler and measure the distance to figure out the timing. Next you would look for hotels in the area so you could call ahead to make reservations. Yikes, that was a lot of work. Now we can program in the coordinates in our smartphone and it will tell us the route, the mileage, the time to destination and we can even search for hotels and restaurants along the route. All without leaving our seat! Technology is an awesome thing. So, with a few tools, you can get started on your map to your goals.

Step 1: Find others who have done what you want to do and copy how they did it.

Step 2: Create your own map. Don't let a lack of tools stop you. You can always use a pencil and paper!

Step 3: Put it on the calendar. Something magical happens when you put something on your calendar. It gets done!

Step 4: Review your map, confirm you are still on track and adjust accordingly.

"Copy, Create, Calendar and Confirm." Now do it. Then do it again! Make it happen!

Weekly Score Sheet

Because we believe we should strive to touch on every element every day we created a simple and effective tool, the *7F Words™ For Living a Balanced Life - Weekly Score Sheet*. The score sheet helps you plan and keep track of your daily accomplishments. You can download it from our website at www.7FWords.com/downloads or simply draw a grid with the days of the week across the top and the seven F Words listed along the left hand column. Leave enough space in each box to write a couple of words that represent the action you took in that category for that day.

The goal is to enter some action that you took for each of the 7F Words™ every day. For example, on Monday you might enter "Oath" in the Focus box because you recited the oath and committed to focus on balance for the day. In the Faith box you might write "Affirmation" or "Prayer". For Family you could note that you spent an extra ten minutes reading to your child. For Finance your actions can be as small as clipping a coupon and using it or signing up to put an extra $100.00 into your savings account every month. Perhaps you parked in the furthest parking

13

space at the grocery store just to walk a few extra steps. That action would go under Fitness. Give yourself a point for each box you marked. Total your points at the bottom of the sheet to get your score for the day.

It's amazing how the small actions you take can have a significant impact on the fulfillment you feel every day. Make every day a "7" and remember to celebrate your successes!

7F Words™ For Living a Balanced Life Daily Score Sheet

	MONDAY	TUESDAY	WEDNESDAY	THURSDAY	FRIDAY	SATURDAY	SUNDAY
FOCUS	Prioritized To Do List	Recited 7 F Words Oath					
FAITH	Gratitude Journal	Said Affirmations					
FREEDOM	Said no without guilt	Cleared my desk					
FAMILY	Dinner with the boys	Called Brother					
FINANCE	Paid credit cards – no interest	Used coupons at grocery store					
FITNESS	Walked 2 miles	Exercised 20 minutes					
FUN	Maxx to the dog park	Words with Friends					
SCORE	7	7					

www.7FWords.com

• • • • • • •

Power Strategy #1: Set Goals That You Are Passionate About

Whatever methods you use to achieve your goal, remember that a key ingredient to success is passion. If you're not passionate about what you're trying to achieve, then perhaps it's time to take a step back and revisit your purpose.

Every one of us is given the same 1,440 minutes in a day. We hope you will use that valuable time to discover what is really important, decide to let go of what is not, and focus on the things that add value and joy to your life.

What is your purpose?

What are you passionate about?

What power strategies can you implement to achieve success?

What will it feel like when you achieve your goals?

"Two are better than one, because they have a good reward for their labor. For if they fall, the one will lift up his fellow; but woe to him that is alone when he falleth, and hath not another to lift him up".

Ecclesiastes 4: 9-10.

*I will have **Faith** in my ability to succeed in all I do.*

"Now faith is the substance of things hoped for, the evidence of things not seen."
Hebrews 11:1

Chapter 2

Faith

"Faith is taking the first step even when you don't see the whole staircase."
Martin Luther King, Jr.

The Right, The Wisdom and The Power

Faith is the dialogue we have with ourselves. Whatever we believe and have faith in will guide our actions. Possessing faith is a critical element that sets people who succeed apart from those who do not. Faith allows us to accept the obstacles that are thrown in our path and have the courage to move forward in spite of fear and adversity. Faith gives us the ability to envision and do what we might otherwise think is impossible. Our faith gives us the courage to believe that we have the right, the wisdom and the power we need to succeed.

What I Learned From a Squirrel

Pastor J.R. Jones of St. Paul Lutheran Church in Boca Raton, Florida tells this story about faith.

A grandfather and his grandson were sitting on a bench watching a squirrel in a tree. The squirrel was in a precarious position at the end of a branch.

The grandfather saw this as a teachable moment and told his grandson, "Watch that squirrel and then tell me what you learn from it."

All of a sudden the squirrel looked like he was going to make an impossible leap to a branch in another tree very far from where he was. He made the leap but landed short of his goal on a branch below.

The grandfather asked, "So what did you learn from the squirrel?"

The boy replied, "Well, maybe he should have stayed there."

"Sometimes life is like that, it's kind of shaky and uncertain. What else did you learn?" asked the grandfather.

The boy responded, "He did jump, but he didn't land where he was trying to get to; he landed on the branch below it."

"Sometimes you have to take that leap of faith. Sometimes you don't land where you thought you would," the grandfather said.

"So you still have some work to do to get where you want to be?"

"That's right," said the grandfather, "What if the squirrel had missed completely? What if he had landed on the ground?"

"It might hurt. But he could get back up, climb the tree and try again. I guess if the squirrel had stayed where he was, then he never would have made it to the other tree at all."

Pastor Jones says he doesn't think God expects us to make "leaps" of faith. He believes in "steps" of faith. Take the next step, believe in the work you are doing and be courageous, so you can get to your goal.

A Leap of Faith
Cathy

In most situations it's the small steps we take each day that eventually get us to the end goal, but I believe there are times when a leap of faith is the only thing that will get us moving. My leap of faith began one Sunday morning when I was attending service in a little Church of the Nazarene in Lehigh Acres, Florida. I was with my husband, Jim, and my parents when it came to me that we should adopt a child. I heard a voice deep in my mind that clearly said, "Adopt a child." It was not the same as the Pastor's voice that was coming from the podium, but something very deep and gently

21

commanding. This was a very unique experience for me and the only time in my life that it had happened.

That was at the end of 1990 and Jim and I had been married for just a little over a year. I was trying to get pregnant and was having no success. Around the same time a dear friend of mine, who already had a son, was also trying to conceive.

One day shortly after I heard "the voice" she and I were discussing our situations and my friend said that she was considering adopting. She suggested that I look into it and gave me the contact information for Universal Aid for Children, an adoption agency in Miami. I called them a few days later and was told that they would be holding their January monthly meeting for families and potential parents the following Friday night. Jim and I decided to go, just to gather information.

The monthly meetings were an opportunity for parents and children in various stages of adoption to learn more about the adoption process and to get to know others in the same situation. There must have been a hundred people at that first meeting Jim and I went to. We met people who were contemplating adoption, as well as many people who had already adopted and had their babies and toddlers in tow. The Director gave an update of the current international adoption process, introduced people who had recently adopted, and then mentioned that she had pictures of children from Romania who were in need of a forever family.

After the meeting Jim and I wandered over to the table that held the pictures. One picture of an adorable little boy stood out. He was about seven years old and had the sweetest expression. It was as though he was reaching out to us to become his parents. When the Director came over to greet us, we asked if he was really available for adoption. She said yes and asked where we were in our "process." We both looked at her and said, "What process?" We were only there to begin thinking about adoption. We hadn't even explored any other options for beginning our family.

After she stepped away we deliberated for a short time and agreed that we should pursue this child. Both Jim and I are well educated people who use good judgment and generally do our research and weigh the facts before making a major decision. What possessed us to decide to adopt this little boy so quickly can be seen as naiveté or even insanity, but I prefer to view it as faith.

We proceeded to tell the Director that we were interested in adopting this little boy. She looked at us as if we were crazy, but humored us anyway by handing us an application packet. That packet contained what seemed to be endless forms. Over the weekend Jim and I filled out all the necessary documents, added income tax returns, bank statements, copies of our passports and various other pieces of information. We needed letters of recommendation, sets of fingerprints and had to be tested for HIV.

By Tuesday afternoon we had our completed packet ready to be overnighted to Miami.

Over the next few weeks while we were working with the agency to pursue our little boy, we began to discuss our plans with our family and friends. Some of them tried to dissuade us. They brought up all the negative things that could come of adopting a child from another country; for example, we didn't even speak the same language. We ignored the negatives and kept pursuing our little boy.

Then one day we received a call telling us that his biological parents had taken him out of the orphanage and he was no longer available for adoption. Our hearts sank. We were happy that he would no longer be in an orphanage but we felt devastated by the loss. We had just experienced a taste of the heartbreak that people told us comes with adoption.

Shortly thereafter we got a call from a sister adoption agency in New Mexico. They were given our telephone number by Universal Aid for Children. The woman on the other end of the phone said that she was representing two Romanian boys, ages 4 and 8, whose mother could no longer care for them. She asked if we were interested in learning more about them and offered to send us a short video of them.

Only a few short weeks before, we were two busy career people who were just "maybe" contemplating adoption. While we were waiting for the video, we talked about the possibility of two children and came to the conclusion that once we adopted one we would probably want to adopt another. So why not do it all at once and keep the brothers together?

Since our boys were not infants we weren't required to go to Romania to pick them up. The agency arranged for a chaperone to accompany them to New York. On May 19, 1991, we found ourselves at JFK Airport waiting to welcome our two sons to their new home and into our hearts. Today our sons Michael and Patrick, ages 30 and 27, have grown into wonderful young men who have enriched our lives from day one. I am thankful that we didn't listen to the people who told us we were crazy to consider adopting from another country. We took a leap of faith; we've never looked back and have absolutely no regrets.

Strengthen Your Faith Muscle

Like the muscles in our bodies our faith needs to be exercised to remain strong. Whether our faith comes from within ourselves, our relationships with others, our faith in God or a combination of all of these elements, it needs constant attention.

Simply having faith doesn't make something happen. If there is something that you desire deeply then you must believe that it can be yours. Once you accept that what you want is possible, you must throw off all your doubts and fears and move forward toward your dream. You have to put your faith into action. Faith without action is just a daydream.

Sometimes you allow old hurts, doubts and fears to hold you back. Now is the time to stop dwelling on the mistakes and hurts of the past and to take positive steps toward a better future. You must treat each and every day as a new beginning and believe in the old saying, "Today is the first day of the rest of your life."

Reciting affirmations on a daily basis can have a tremendous impact on the way you view yourself and those around you. Affirmations are a positive declaration of a truth. They are short statements that when repeated can target and undermine damaging negative beliefs. The purpose is to replace the negative beliefs with positive beliefs that propel you toward more positive and rewarding actions.

Here are some affirmations you might try:

- I believe in myself and my ability to succeed.

- I have a caring support network that has my best interest at heart.

- Success and achievement come naturally to me.

- My faith in God is the cornerstone of my existence and I live my life in goodness and love.

Having faith and trust in others is an important component for success. The ability to rely on and be led by others is not

26

always easy, but no one can succeed in a vacuum. You need other people to listen to you, to support you, to advise and guide you. It's very easy to get discouraged by negative people and influences around you. Surround yourself with people and things that will provide positive influences and motivations.

Instead of watching negative news, reach for something motivational that will put you in a positive frame of mind. Replace your old thoughts and reprogram your mind with uplifting and motivating material.

The Power of Prayer
Deborah

Prayer is my conversation with God. It is what I do to strengthen my faith on a daily basis. It is how I start my day, become focused and ready to take on the challenges that are thrown my way. But prayer is not something I have been doing all my life.

My children attended a small Christian school during their elementary and middle school years. There was a group of moms who got together once a month to pray for the students, the school and the requests that came in from the teachers. I was invited to attend but was reluctant since I didn't really know how to pray, let alone pray out loud or pray for someone else. So I decided to go and simply observe. During that first encounter I learned that it didn't really matter that I didn't know how to pray. Praying was simply a way of expressing gratitude, specific concerns and desires.

The structure of this group was loosely based on Moms in Touch, now called Moms in Prayer. This organization reaches out to mothers all over the world and teaches them how to blanket their children's lives and schools in prayer. Their mission is to impact children in schools worldwide for Christ by gathering mothers to pray. The organization promotes using a template for prayer:

- Praise God

- Confess your sins

- Give thanks

- Pray on behalf of others

We confidentially prayed for all the students' requests; everything from a sick gerbil to a terminally ill parent. The most fulfilling aspect of this process was hearing from parents and students about how their prayers were answered.

Because I had such a good experience with the elementary and middle school prayer groups, I searched out a high school Moms in Prayer group. It gave me much needed peace on more than one occasion to know that people kept us in their prayers.

When my son Michael was in high school he went with his class on a five-day mission trip to Costa Rica. The purpose of the trip was to help build a community center and church for people who were living in cardboard and tin huts. All the while he was there I prayed that he and everyone on the trip would remain safe and return home unharmed.

On the day he came home I went to the school to pick him up. One of the chaperones pulled me aside and told me about a hair-raising experience. As a reward for their hard work the students went on a white-water rafting excursion. She described how Michael had fallen out of the raft and was sucked under the water. He was rapidly being pulled away by the current. The rafting guide, a very small man, reached his pole under Michael's life vest and with one swift motion, flipped my 6'3" son back into the raft. The chaperone described the incident as nothing short of a miracle.

I look back on that incident with gratitude that the guide was given the strength to act quickly and pull Michael from peril. I could have lost my son that day. I believe he was spared because God has bigger plans for him.

Prayer has made a significant impact on my life. It has made me a more thankful person. I start and end each day in prayer, with an attitude of gratitude. I find myself praying all day long, in every imaginable situation. Prayer keeps me focused. It shapes my thoughts and actions and helps me get through the tough times with grace and courage. It has brought me into a more fulfilling personal relationship with God that I treasure. Several people I know keep a prayer journal and when they reread it sometime later they're amazed at how their prayers have been answered.

You Never Know
Cathy

Being a Real Estate Agent is often like being on an emotional roller coaster. There are so many ups and downs. When you find the perfect house for a buyer there is a tremendous sense of elation; however, if for some reason the deal falls through it can be emotionally and financially devastating. If you're a Real Estate Agent or any type of sales professional who works on a commission basis, and you're not careful, you can let these emotional highs and lows take a tremendous negative toll on all aspects of your life.

One of my favorite stories is one about a Chinese farmer that was circulating around the internet several years ago. This little story has shaped my attitude about so many of the things that happen in my life. It has helped me keep a positive outlook even when circumstances seem hopeless. The story goes like this:

Long ago there was a Chinese farmer who had one son and one horse. One day his horse broke loose and ran away. On hearing this, his neighbor came by and said, "Your horse is gone, what bad luck."

"Why?" asked the farmer, "How do you know it is bad luck?"

The next day the horse returned, bringing a herd of horses with him. The farmer's son locked them all in the corral and now the farmer had many horses. The neighbor came back and exclaimed, "Oh, how fortunate you are to have so many horses!"

The farmer simply asked, "How do you know that's good fortune?"

Several days later the son was trying to break one of the horses and was thrown off and broke his leg. Once again the neighbor came by and upon seeing the son said, "Oh, what terrible luck."

Again the farmer replied, "How do you know that it's terrible luck?"

Shortly afterwards a warlord came through the small town. He took away all of the able-bodied young men, enlisting them into battle. Sadly, those young men never returned. The farmer's son however, was spared because of his broken leg.

The moral of the story is that no one really knows if a particular incident is good or bad. Only time will tell. Sometimes we have to look back to realize why we had to go through the experiences we did.

Is there a situation in your life that at the moment seems terrible? Could it be that it turns out to be the best thing that has ever happened to you? Is there something that you can do to turn that negative situation into something positive for yourself or for someone else? The universe has a way of giving you what you expect. You don't know what tomorrow will bring, so have faith that things will work out for the best.

Gratitude Journal

Deborah

How can you use your faith in God, in the world or in yourself to your advantage every day? To begin with, take inventory of all the things for which you are grateful. Your list could include things as simple as a comfy bed or a smile from a loved one.

In her show on Mastering the Art of Gratitude with Lifeclass teachers Iyanla Vanzant, Tony Robbins, Bishop T.D. Jakes and Deepak Chopra, Oprah Winfrey said, "What I know for sure is that no matter what is going on in your life I believe if you concentrate on what you have you always wind up having more..." She goes on to say, "If you focus on what you don't have you will never ever, ever have enough." She believes that starting a gratitude journal is the single most important thing she has done.

Apply your attitude of gratitude to every day by writing down at least five things for which you are grateful. Simply saying them to yourself or someone else is not enough. If you're not the type to pick up a pen and write in a journal then there's an app for that. A word of caution though; make sure that your app is saving your journal or that you're downloading it to a secure place. Your gratitude journal is something you will definitely want to go back and reread from time to time.

Start each day with an attitude of gratitude. It will be fun to see what that does for the rest of your day. You may want to get started and use the space below to jot down a few things for which you are grateful.

Eat Every Day

Cathy

Shortly after Jim and I adopted our boys and they began to grasp the English language we thought it would be a good idea to bring them to a child psychologist. Michael had been acting out a bit and we wanted some professional advice on child rearing. During the patient intake the doctor asked Michael what he liked most about being in America. Without hesitation he looked the doctor square in the eyes and said emphatically, in his limited English, "Eat every day." Those three little words brought tears to our eyes. It became evident that in Romania, Michael didn't get to eat every day. He lived in squalor and competed for food with nine or ten other family members. Most of us in the U.S. don't know what it is to go hungry for more than a few hours. For me, those three little words have brought a much more profound meaning to the prayer, "Bless us O Lord and these Thy gifts..."

First Class

Barbara

I was looking forward to my trip to Australia. As I boarded the plane I took note of the passengers sitting in first class and thought to myself, "Someday I want to ride first class." After sitting uncomfortably in the back of the plane for over fifteen hours I started praying, "Dear Lord, please let me ride first class next time!"

Every year we take a train trip from California to Texas, to visit my husband Dave's family. We arrive at Union Station in Los Angeles and marvel at the architecture of the place with sky high ceilings, tile and the beautiful iron work with that Art Deco feel from the 1920s. Every time we see it in the movies or on TV we say, "We've been there!"

On our last trip back from Texas there was a huge snow storm between Dallas and Chicago so our train was delayed. We called and called the train station but they kept telling us not to hurry because the train was still not at the station. We called one last time and to our dismay they told us, "Oh, the train just left the station." Oh my! Now what? We had just missed our train. Dave's dad came to the rescue. He lent us his truck so we could drive to San Antonio and catch the train from there.

When we boarded the train the attendants were so gracious and apologetic that we had missed the train because of the miscommunication at the station. As a token of their apology, they upgraded us to a "first class" sleeper. It was amazing. It had a big bed and our own little bathroom so we didn't have to share. I realized my prayer had been answered, I was riding First Class! It was not exactly what I had in mind at the time of the prayer but it sure was nice and it made me realize that even our smallest prayers can be answered.

· · · · · · · ·

Power Strategy #2: Adopt an Attitude of Faith

Embrace a new attitude of faith in a future that is better than your past. Once you believe that a brighter future is possible and can envision the results, it can become your reality. Start charting your course, come up with a plan, then have faith that anything is possible if you believe.

Follow the example from the story *What I Learned from a Squirrel*: To get from here to there you have to take a leap, or at least a step of faith.

How can you start each day with a new slate?

What changes can you make to have the life you want?

What can you do to exercise your faith muscle?

"Faith is to believe what you do not see: the reward of this faith is to see what you believe."
Saint Augustine

"Faith is a knowledge within the heart, beyond the reach of proof.
Khalil Gibran

"Do not conform any longer to the pattern of this world, but be transformed by the renewing of your mind. Then you will be able to test and approve what God's will is – his good, pleasing and perfect will."
Romans 12:2

"If you think you can, or you think you can't, you are right."
Henry Ford

"Faith is believing in something when common sense tells you not to."
From the movie Miracle on 34th Street.

*I will allow myself the **<u>Freedom</u>** to say no to things I do not want to do or that will not advance me toward my goals.*

Freedom: the power to determine action without restraint

Random House Webster's College Dictionary

Chapter 3

Freedom

"For to be free is not merely to cast off one's chains, but to live in a way that respects and enhances the freedom of others."
Nelson Mandela

An acquaintance of Barbara's from Afghanistan came to the United States several years ago with his wife and children. One beautiful spring day he caught sight of his wife driving down the street. She had her arm out the window, the wind was blowing her hair and she had a big smile on her face. The beautiful sight of her made him cry with joy because when they were in Afghanistan she would not have been able to enjoy the warmth of the sun on her skin and the wind in her hair while in a public place.

As American citizens freedom comes naturally to us. We breathe it in and out like oxygen. We need it and as long as it is readily available we don't notice it much. However, if our liberties were threatened we would certainly take notice and fight to maintain them. We live in a great country, founded by brave people who fought and died so we could have our freedom.

Our Declaration of Independence asserts "… that all men are created equal, that they are endowed by their Creator with certain unalienable Rights, that among these are Life, Liberty and the pursuit of Happiness." Along with these rights comes responsibility. We have a responsibility to protect our rights and liberties and we also have a responsibility to use them for good. One way we can exercise and protect our freedom is to use it to enhance the balance in our lives. With balance comes greater productivity, enjoyment and fulfillment.

From the time American children are very young they are told they can be anything they want to be. Our children are encouraged to explore the endless possibilities of who they can become when they grow up. "What do you want to be when you grow up?" is a question our children are so commonly asked.

Who have you become? Are you fully exercising your rights to life, liberty and the pursuit of happiness? Are you paying respect to the American forefathers by taking full advantage of your freedoms every day?

Free as a Bird

You can make the most of your freedom by integrating it into the other *7F Words™*: Focus, Faith, Family, Finance, Fitness and Fun. You can plan your day so you can <u>Focus</u> on the activities that make you happy and help you reach your goals.

Freedom also allows you to say no to the things that don't fit in your plan or that you just don't have any desire to do. You don't have to feel guilty about saying "no." Barbara has "Just Say No" parties on her back porch. She and her friends sit outside, watch the sunset with a nice cocktail and practice saying "No," "NO," "NOOOOO!"

If you find your career is not fulfilling or providing you with what you need, you can develop a long range plan to switch to a career that will enrich your life. Barbara appreciates the lack of restrictions that owning her own firm offers her. She has the freedom to plan her day around her family commitments and the flexibility to be home with her teenage sons when they need her.

You have the right to decide whether or not to practice a religion and the freedom to put your <u>Faith</u> in whatever it is that will help you become your finest self. You have the freedom to create the <u>Family</u> relationships you desire. Your "family" might include adopted children, your co-workers, neighbors, friends or extended family.

Most of us strive in some way for <u>Financial</u> freedom. The majority of us must be gainfully employed to pay for what we need. We sometimes lose sight of the difference between what we need and what we want. Taking a realistic view of what we actually need and what we do not can be extremely freeing both mentally and financially.

Make good choices today so that you are ready for whatever tomorrow brings. One of Barbara's clients is a real estate agent. She said the downturn in the real estate market did not impact her as much as it did many other real estate agents. She has no debt, her house is paid for, she drives an older, but nice car and she does not have a fancy office. She could handle the downturn and it did not destroy her financially because she made good choices a long time ago.

Negative influences are poisonous to our physical and mental well-being. We have the freedom to weed the negatives out of our lives, just like a farmer who plants a field. He knows that weeds will choke his crop and suck the valuable nutrients from the soil. So every day he goes out with a hoe and chops out the weeds. Are you weeding out the negative influences that are jeopardizing your mental and physical <u>Fitness</u>?

It is profound that our forefathers included the "pursuit of happiness" as an unalienable right in the Declaration of Independence. Everyone is happy when they're having <u>Fun</u>. The words are almost synonymous. Adding a little bit of fun to every day can go a long way to enhancing your sense of freedom and well-being.

42

You can see that freedom integrates with every other F word. Work on your *7F Words*™ so that you can move toward a greater sense of balance. Keep the negatives at bay. Exercise your faith and go do the things that are important to you.

Freedom from Clutter

Barbara

We have to make room for the good things in our life. If our home is full of stuff, our garage is full of stuff, our closets are full of stuff and our desk is covered with stuff, then we don't have room for the good things, the important things; the things that will bring the most meaning to our lives.

I was inspired by Dale Manno of Dale Designs in Boynton Beach, Florida when Deborah and Cathy interviewed her on WRPBiTV. The topic was Freedom from Clutter. I took a look around my home office and knew it was time. I made a pile for "keep", "donate" and "trash". I was ruthless. If it was not needed, or didn't have some sentimental value, it had to go. I had a car load for our local women's shelter, boxes of books for the used book store, and several bags of trash. Now I had the space I needed to organize the remainder. No more "vertical filing" or stacks on my desk. I made a place in a file cabinet for all of my important papers, such as wills, power of attorney, investment accounts, etc. I emptied out the inbox that was supposed to be for items that needed my attention such as bills and bank statements. I created a project drawer where I can keep up with the latest inspiration that I'm working on. I'm a firm believer in only having one project at a time on my desk. What a good feeling to walk into my office now. I can sit at my desk and get to work right away. I'm no longer sorting through "stuff" to get to what I need. I've made room for the good things.

Dale heard about my home office makeover and sent us this message: "Barbara's comments represent the best possible outcome from an organizing consultation. By investing the time to increase efficiency in her home office during her sort, purge, and organizing session, she was able to:

- Save time
- Promote recycling
- Support her local women's shelter
- Benefit the used book store
- RELAX!

Each of my consulting clients is furnished with a personalized suggested plan of action. Barbara created her own, with a very positive result...freedom from clutter!"

. . . .

Power Strategy #3: Just Say No

Today is the perfect day to declare your freedom. Take action. Ruthlessly prioritize your time. Give yourself license to say no, without guilt, to the things that don't fit your plan. Download your own copy of License To Say "No" at www.7FWords.com.

What does freedom mean to you?

What do you want to be free from?

What do you want to be free to do?

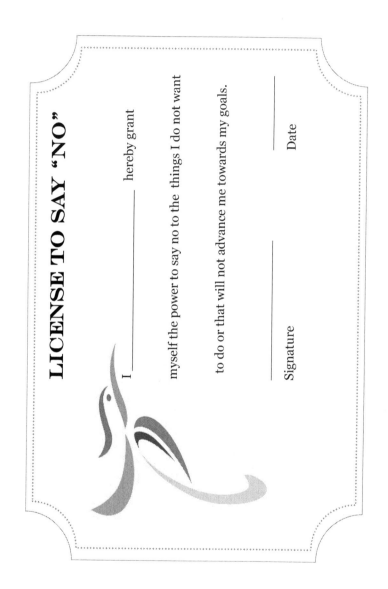

LICENSE TO SAY "NO"

I _____ hereby grant myself the power to say no to the things I do not want to do or that will not advance me towards my goals.

_____
Signature

_____
Date

"Freedom is not worth having if it does not include the freedom to make mistakes."
Mahatma Gandhi

"But whoever looks intently into the perfect law that gives freedom, and continues in it—not forgetting what they have heard, but doing it—they will be blessed in what they do."
James 1:25

*I will spend time nurturing my relationships with my **Family** and those who are important to me.*

Copyright © 2013 by Tom Gnadinger Photography

Family: Any group of persons closely related by blood; a group of people who are generally not blood relations but who share common attitudes, interests or goals

Random House Webster's College Dictionary

Chapter 4

Family

"Sister is probably the most competitive relationship within the family, but once the sisters are grown, it becomes the strongest relationship."

Margaret Mead

The desire for social and interpersonal interaction is a fundamental human motivation. It's imperative to our well-being to feel a sense of belonging. Our ancestors tended to stay in the same geographic location for generations and generations. They raised their families in the same town where they grew up. Extended families got together regularly. Children grew up with cousins who were close in age and proximity. Grandparents often lived in the same house or on the same street as their grandchildren and if not, they saw them as often as possible.

Today it's very common for children to go away to college, find jobs and settle down in places that are quite far away from their parents, siblings and other blood relations. This phenomenon can be damaging to one's sense of belonging. It's important to somehow fill the void that is created when separated from family by long distances.

In this book we refer to Family as those people who make a positive difference in each other's lives. In addition to our blood relatives, immediate family members and significant others, these people may be co-workers, close friends, classmates, teachers, mentors, religious affiliates, business affiliates, sports team members or anyone with whom we share common goals. These are the people to whom we are most emotionally tied. We bring each other pleasure, pain, happiness, sadness, love and virtually every other emotion imaginable.

We so often hear people say that "Family comes first". Yet, in this dynamic age in which we live, we often find ourselves too busy to spend quality time nurturing our most important relationships. There are only twenty-four hours in a day and we spend one-third of those sleeping. Most of us spend at least another eight hours working. Every day there are people vying for our precious time. If we're to achieve balance in our lives we must use the time we have to focus on our family and friends. We need to let go of people or activities that prevent us from paying attention to the people who really matter.

Who are the people or groups of people who comprise your most important relationships? Most people can think of at least seven people or groups in their life who are critically important. We refer to them as your "Significant 7". Take a moment to make a list of the seven people or groups you feel are most significant in your life. Once you've listed them please ask yourself if those are the people to whom you are giving the most of yourself. Are your Significant 7 getting their fair share of your time and energy or are they only getting what's left over after the end of your busy day?

Now take a moment to list the major activities in your life using our Significant 7 Worksheet (available online at www.7FWords.com/free-downloads) Like many, your list might include work, school, church, sports, entertainment, hobbies, volunteer work, networking, time with friends, etc. Think about how much time your Significant 7 are included in those activities. If the answer is very little, then your relationships and activities are most likely not in balance. How can you adjust your activities or schedules to include or make more time for your Significant 7?

7F WORDS™ SIGNIFICANT 7 WORKSHEET

SIGNIFICANT 7	MAJOR ACTIVITIES	COMMENTS
	HOME	
JIM	Meals	Have more meals at home.
	Household Chores	
	Refurbishing	
MIKE	WORK/VOLUNTEER	
	Real Estate Work	
	Certified Sisters Work	
PAT	Homeowner's Association	
CERTIFIED	Global Business Alliance	
SISTERS	SOCIAL/FUN	
	Movies	
	Words With Friends	
	TV	Less TV, read more.
ELLEN	Dancing	
	Dog Park	
DONNA	FITNESS	
	Walks	
	Strength Training	Get workout buddy.
MAXX		

Your *Significant 7* can be a very dynamic group and may change often. At any given point in time you may find that one member of your *Significant 7* requires you to spend the lion's share of your time with them. What happens then to the other six?

Every choice you make with regard to the *7F Words™* ultimately comes back to affect your family. It can sometimes be overwhelming to give everyone who needs your attention the time they deserve and still keep yourself in good health physically and mentally. If all your *7F Words™* are in balance you'll be much better prepared to deal with a family crisis should one arise. If you weed out the people or activities that are unimportant and usurping your time you will find yourself with more time to devote to your important relationships.

Take another look at your *Significant 7* list. How many of these people are supporting your needs? We rely on these people to provide us with love and emotional support. If someone on your list is not providing something positive to the relationship should they really be on the list? Are they worthy of your precious time? Are they taking the place of someone else who is ready, willing and able to provide you with what you need? These questions can be very difficult to answer, to say the least, but are definitely worth exploring.

There may come a time when you're more sensitive to your need to belong. If there is a void in your *Significant 7* list, then it's time to fill that void. It's important to believe that whatever familial, community or supportive relationship you desire is within your reach. But, it's up to you to take the initiative to make it happen. There has never been a more exciting time for single people to meet someone with whom they can have a meaningful relationship. Meet-up groups, internet dating services, and match-making services are plentiful. If you're looking for love it is out there to be found.

In the chapter on Faith, Cathy shared the story of how she and her husband Jim created their family through the adoption of older children from another country. Deborah and her husband Michael also adopted their three children; two lovely daughters and a wonderful son who came to them as infants.

Family Traditions

Barbara

Family means something a little different to each of us. Growing up, mine was traditional, in that I had a mother and father, brothers and sisters.   I was the youngest of eight siblings. Christmas, Thanksgiving and Easter were big at my house. Everyone came. My older brothers and sisters who were married brought their spouses and children.   Many of their children were near my age so I always had someone to play with. Everyone brought a dish and there was always tons of food. My favorite was my sister Joan's chocolate cream pie!

Now I am married and have children of my own. As a military family we move every few years and live very far from our families. Our military community of friends has become our "family." And we have made our own family traditions. In our case we invite the single sailors and solo families from the Navy base to our house for Thanksgiving. Everyone brings a dish, usually a traditional family favorite. So, I still have a house full of people, lots of food and football. Family is what you make it. If you don't have a family you might invite someone special to dinner or volunteer at a soup kitchen. Create your own family traditions.

To Have or Not to Have?

Deborah

Michael and I got married when I was nineteen and he was twenty-nine. For the first couple of years of our marriage we didn't think much about starting a family. We were very involved in our own careers. We were having fun. Our money went toward vacations and new toys. At some point when I was in my twenties I began trying to get pregnant. After a few years of no success we went to a fertility specialist; the prognosis was not hopeful so we accepted the fact that we might never have children.

One day a friend was showing off her new diamond bracelet. She explained that it was a gift from her husband in an attempt to keep her happy because he didn't want to have children even though she desperately wanted a family. The sadness in her eyes was so intense and overwhelming that even after all these years I can still remember her sorrowful look.

We convinced ourselves that if we could not have children of our own then we probably were not meant to have them. Michael and I just continued working hard and enjoyed living the life we were living. Adoption was not something we had considered until my friend, Sue, asked me to watch her newly adopted baby boy while she took her other son to a class. The moment I held that infant something happened and I knew that I could love a baby, adopted or not.

Thus began our adoption journey. After some ups and downs in the road we were eventually blessed with three amazing children. I thank God every day for them and for their birth mothers who had the courage to plan a future for their babies that included me.

· · · · · · ·

Power Strategy #4: Focus on Your Significant 7

When Barbara was a manager for KPMG, one of the "Big Six" accounting firms, they sent her to their management training program. For Barbara the most memorable thing they said was "KPMG won't be there to wipe the drool from your chin, so you better take care of your family. It is not all about the job."

Who are the most important people in your life?

What actions are you taking to support your significant relationships?

How are you spending your valuable time?

Who will miss you when you're gone?

"When your mother asks, 'Do you want a piece of advice?' it's a mere formality. It doesn't matter if you answer yes or no. You're going to get it anyway."
Erma Bombeck

"What can you do to promote world peace? Go home and love your family."
Mother Teresa

*I will be conscious of my **Finances** and act accordingly.*

Finance: The monetary resources of a company, individual or government

Random House Webster's College Dictionary

Chapter 5

Finance

What can be added to the happiness of a man who is in health, out of debt, and has a clear conscience?
Adam Smith

Control the Money

Barbara

Money is like water from the faucet. Whether there is a little trickle or it is on full force, if you don't put the stopper in the sink it all goes down the drain. So let's talk about how to turn the trickle into a full-on flow and how to control the outflow so you can decide if and when to take the stopper out.

In this chapter we'll discuss developing a plan for your finances. We'll talk about how to control the inflow, or the income and how to control the outflow, or the spending once you have a steady stream of income. Controlling the outflow or expenses is always a challenge. Debt is a way to have inflow and outflow but it comes at a great price, so we'll talk about controlling debt. Finally, we'll look at ways to teach our children about money.

The Plan

First things first, what's your plan? Let's start with a list. I want you to put everything you can think of on the list that you want in the next 5 years, 10 years, and 20 years. It might look like this:

5 Years: Pay off my new car

Save the down payment for my first house

Start our family

Put the maximum amount in my IRA

Donate 10% to my church per year

Take a trip to Hawaii

10 Years: Purchase a new car

Build a pool in the backyard

Donate 10% to my church per year

Put the maximum amount in my 401k plan

Set up a college fund for my children

Take a trip to Italy

20 Years: Have my house paid off

Donate 10% to my church per year

Put the maximum amount in my 401k plan

Watch my children graduate from college

Travel Europe

Those are the big picture goals. Now you will need to break them down into what I call "chewable chunks." You've heard the question, "How do you eat an elephant?" The answer is, "One bite at a time." This analogy applies well to our finances. It's the little things we do with our money that get us where we want to be financially. With that in mind let's move on to controlling the inflows and outflows.

Control the Inflow

How much money do you bring home after taxes? That will determine what you have to work with. This is where a lot of people feel trapped; trapped in a job, trapped by mounting debt or trapped by other obligations that use up time. Let's talk about income and how someone might make more money even if they are "trapped."

Let's start with those of us who work for an employer. You could look for another job that pays more. You could take some courses to improve skills that are valuable to your employer. You could take on extra assignments that make you more valuable.

You could get a degree. With all the resources available online it is easier than ever to gain new skills and education.

I've seen some very skilled craftspeople set up an online store and do very well either with their own product or with someone else's product. There are many sources for hosting online stores such as Etsy, Yahoo or GoDaddy.com. You can set up an online payment option through PayPal or other merchant service account. Now you have what I call "mailbox money." And if you automate the online store you can make money while you sleep. Check out our Favorite Resources page at www.7FWords.com/Favorite-Resources for links to other resources for your online business.

Setting up a small business on the side is another way to increase income. For example, you might be an awesome musician. What if you gave lessons? I've seen this taken a step further, leverage the lessons by creating a student "band." That way instead of having one student at a time you could have four or five at a time. Now you're getting creative!

What about your investments? I don't give investment advice but I do seek investment advice. There are several types of advisors; those who sell a product such as IRAs, CDs, and Annuities, independent financial planners and wealth managers. I tend to like the independent financial planners because they will look at the entire financial picture and help set up a plan to reach your investment goals. They charge a fee for their services. It helps them be a little more interested in what is best for you.

Make a list of all sources of income or cash inflow and add up the total. Let's use $100,000 for example, less $20,000 for taxes leaves you with $80,000. Now divide that number by 2,000 hours, roughly the number of work hours a year based on a 40 hour work week and two weeks of vacation. That equates to roughly $40 per hour worked. This is the starting point for your plan. Keep this number in mind. We'll use it again later. Now let's look at controlling your outflow.

Control the Outflow

One of the most useful ways to get control of your finances is to track every penny you spend. You might use a computer program or a spreadsheet. Or if you are not comfortable with those types of systems you can set up a simple file system. Make a folder for each type of expense that you normally have; one for loans, one for charitable donations, one for gas and groceries, one for entertainment, etc. Put every receipt in a folder and at the end of the month add them up. Then make a list of each type and write down the totals. Do this every month and lay the lists side by side, you'll be shocked to realize what you're actually spending

Look for ways to decrease your spending. This could be to renegotiate or refinance debt at a lower interest rate or shop for a better rate on insurance. You could brown bag your lunch rather than eating out, which is also a good way to eat better for Fitness. Instead of going out to a movie you could have a movie night at home. Check out *Seven under Seven* in the Fun chapter for other inexpensive ways to have fun on a budget. Take a look at what you're spending and compare that to your plan. Does it fit?

One of my clients told me the story of her single mother who was a waitress. Her mother kept a jar under her bed and every night she would put her tip money in the jar. Once a year they would drive from California to Arizona to her aunt's house to visit family and go shopping for school clothes. This was the highlight of her year as a child. She remembered how her mother was able to stretch her paycheck and save for that trip.

Deborah told us about her mother-in-law and how she had an envelope for each of her monthly bills. When her paycheck came in she would divide it up between the envelopes. That way she always had enough to pay the monthly bills.

When I was a starving college student I would write my monthly bills on the calendar along with the amount my paycheck was going to be. That way I could see how much I needed to set aside from each check. It was tight, but I was able to manage and not go into debt, a topic I feel strongly about.

Whether you use a computer program or a simple folder system, you need to know how your money is being spent so that you can manage it.

Debt

Debt is not an evil word but it can be evil to get out from under. There are reasons to go into debt; a mortgage to buy a home, or a loan to purchase a car. Most people do not need to finance a pair of shoes and a purse. So then why do so many people have thousands of dollars in credit card debt for just that kind of purchase? Credit card companies make it too easy to purchase.

When my husband and I first got married we both worked, we had no children and only a mortgage loan. We were making really good money, yet we had credit card debt. We were the perfect example of the more you make the more you spend. We were a young couple heading down a slippery slope. We sat down together and decided that we wouldn't put any more money on the credit card than we could afford to pay off every month. We were then able to pay off our credit card debt and keep it off by controlling our spending.

Another way to control your spending is to limit yourself to only paying cash for purchases. This works really well, especially if you're at the mall and find the most awesome pair of shoes. It is a lot harder to let go of $300 in cash than to swipe the credit card. Before I let go of my hard earned cash I stop and think, "Do I really need this?" "How many hours do I have to work to pay for this?" Remember the $40 per hour we calculated before? That means you have to work about 7.5 hours to pay for those shoes!

Shopping for the best interest rates for major purchases such as a home loan or car loan will pay the debt down faster. Some mortgage lenders will let you make payments twice a month. On a 30 year fixed loan of $400,000 at 3.75% you would save $31,259 in interest and you would pay off the loan in 25 years rather than 30 years. Not bad for just changing from one payment a month to two.

Pay your loans off early and then use the money you had been paying on the loan to set up a savings account. Set this money aside for your next big purchase such as a new car. Then when you're ready to retire the old clunker you'll have the money to pay cash for that nice new one. What a nice feeling that would be. Plus, you usually get a better deal when you pay with cash.

Teach our Children

Our children need to understand money at an early age. I feel very strongly about giving our children an allowance. Mine get $5 a week. They can spend it however they want. I do this for several reasons.

If they make a poor purchase decision, they have not lost too much money and they learned a valuable lesson. If they want something that costs more than $5 then they need to save for it.

My oldest son wanted a gaming laptop. I told him to save his money and buy one. I could have purchased it for him, but there would have been absolutely no financial lesson in that. Since he really wanted the laptop he found creative ways to earn the money faster.

For over a year he saved his allowance and birthday money; he gathered up the recycling from all the neighbors and cashed that in about once a month. He found odd jobs such as watering the neighbors' plants while they were away. Finally, he had enough to buy the laptop.

He did the research and found a refurbished machine on eBay. I suggested he might want to buy from a known retailer but he was looking for a "deal". So being the "thoughtful and kind" mother that I am, I let him take the risk.

He was so excited the day the computer came, but when he opened it up the worst thing ever happened - it wouldn't even turn on. After many phone calls and emails we were able to return it, but he lost the postage of $31 out of his hard earned savings. Lesson learned; sometimes cheaper is not better. He finally purchased a new computer and has been very pleased with it and proud of himself for his accomplishment.

Please note a few lessons learned here. My son learned to control the inflow of money by getting creative; saving money toward a goal and listening to his mother's advice (I thought this was the most important!). Most of all he learned from his mistake.

Another idea that I like is giving each child three jars to sit on their desk or dresser. Label the jars "Savings" "Spending" and "Giving." You can decide what percentage to put in each jar. Every time they get money from allowance, birthdays, holidays, etc. they must divide it between the jars. You can use envelopes or shoe boxes, whatever works for you. I like the mason jars because you can see the money inside.

When they get $50 in the "Savings" jar it is time to go to the bank and open a child's savings account. They will earn a little interest and most banks do not charge a fee for the "youth" savings account. It's fun to go online and see how much is in the account.

One more thought regarding allowance - they must earn it. There must be a consequence if they don't do what they're supposed to do such as make the bed and pick up their dirty clothes. We have a "deadline" of Sunday evening for their room to be picked up. If the room is not picked up before bedtime then no allowance. It's easy to monitor and easy to enforce. We start off the week with a semi-neat room that seems to carry through most of the week.

By teaching our children early that they must work and save for the things they want, and by not giving them everything they ask for, we set them up for success. They find creative ways to make money, their self-esteem increases because they're able to accomplish a goal all by themselves. Money becomes something tangible and of importance, not just numbers on a page.

• • • • • • •

Power Strategy #5: Control the Inflow and the Outflow

Control your money and you will achieve the financial freedom you've been looking for. Develop a plan for your money, be conscious of your income, spend it according to your plan and save for your future.

Can you envision living your life with financial freedom and security?

What little things can you do every day to improve your financial situation?

What major strategies can you implement to improve your financial situation?

What would it mean to you to be free from debt?

What's your plan for your financial future?

"Your net worth to the world is usually determined by what remains after your bad habits are subtracted from your good ones."
Benjamin Franklin

"Wealth consists not in having great possessions, but in having few wants."
Epictetus

"Starting out to make money is the greatest mistake in life. Do what you have a flare for doing, and if you are good enough at it, the money will come."
Greer Garson

*I will take action to ensure my mental and physical **Fitness**.*

Fitness: The state of having both mental and physical good health

Chapter 6

Fitness

"Physical fitness is not only one of the most important keys to a healthy body; it is the basis of dynamic and creative intellectual activity."
John F. Kennedy

Barbara

Fitness is not just physical well-being, but also mental well-being. Are you self-confident and assured of your ability to perform the daily challenges life throws at you?

I have a ritual, a habit, a routine. I get up the same way and do the same things every morning. I drink the same coffee every day. You may think that's boring, at least that's what my son tells me. He says, "You're so booooring!" I need that routine. It sets me up to accomplish the other things that are not routine. Steven Covey wrote about the *7 Habits of Highly Effective People*. He knew what he was talking about when he called them habits. If we want to be physically and mentally fit then we need to make a habit of the things that help us maintain physical and mental fitness.

I'll tell you how I stay fit so that you can, too. I get up at 5:45 AM every day, get presentable, have my first heavenly cup of coffee, take the boys to school, go to the gym, work out for an hour, get cleaned up, and then go to work. That's it. Don't worry if that schedule doesn't work for you. Come up with a schedule that fits your life. Scheduling is the key, so make sure it goes on your calendar. Since physical fitness is one of my priorities it gets done first thing every day. I make it a habit and I miss it if I can't do it.

Eat the Cookie

Barbara

We are what we eat. A big part of my physical fitness is what I eat. If it goes in my body it better be good for my body and my mind. Now don't think for one minute I count every calorie. I don't, but I do think about it. I read the nutrition labels on everything so I know what I'm eating. And if I want a cookie with my tea in the afternoon, I'm going to have one. Notice I said one and not the whole box. Eat what you want, but eat it in the proper portion size to maintain the weight you want. Restaurants are getting on the nutrition bandwagon and putting calorie content on the menus. It's eye opening and disturbing.

A good source for keeping up with daily calorie intake is the mobile app www.MyFitnessPal.com. I like this one because it has a library of common foods by brand, so I can type in fries and it will tell me the calorie count and add it to my daily log. I can put in my exercise for the day and how many calories I've earned. It totals it all up for me and I can see if I'm on target or if I've overdone it a little

I know I said the food I eat must be good for my body and my mind. I don't know about you, but sometimes I just want a cookie. I like cookies, they make me happy. And if I don't get a cookie I eat everything else in sight trying to satisfy that need for a cookie. If I just eat the cookie in the first place, I consume far fewer calories. The moral is, "Eat the cookie!" Here is a great recipe for a healthy and delicious cookie.

Banana, Oatmeal and Applesauce Cookies

3 Mashed Bananas (ripe)
2 Cups Oatmeal (rolled oats)
1/3 Cup Unsweetened Applesauce
1/3 Cup Almond Milk
1/3 Cup Raisins or Craisins (optional)
1/3 Cup Dark Chocolate Chips (optional)
1 Teaspoon Vanilla
1 Teaspoon Cinnamon

Preheat oven to 350 degrees. Mix bananas, applesauce, almond milk, vanilla and cinnamon until blended. Add oats, raisins and chocolate chips. (Mixture should hold together well enough to drop onto cookie sheet. If not add more oats until mixture is firm enough.) Use a tablespoon to drop onto greased cookie sheet. Cook for 15-20 minutes.

The way I eat is also a habit. On most days I eat the same things. For breakfast I have a cup of coffee with cream and a bowl of oatmeal or a scrambled egg on toast. Then for lunch I have a bowl of soup or a salad. Late in the afternoon I need a pick-me-up so I have my cup of tea and the cookie! I try to make something healthy for our family dinner. I usually have some sort of grilled or baked protein and a vegetable. At the end of the day I have a nice glass of wine. That's it for me. That's my habit. I know it's boring, but it works. And that leaves room for date night on the weekends.

If your habit is to skip breakfast, eat a bacon double cheeseburger and a soda for lunch, then a big meal in the evening followed by a snack in front of the TV, it's time to change your habit. Change the behavior, change the habit. I used to drink a soda every afternoon. Every afternoon! That was a horrible habit. In order to change the habit I had to change the behavior so I started drinking tea. Now when I have that late afternoon slump I have a cup of tea. It took a while, but now I want the tea and not the soda. Ok, I know I need to work on the cookie habit!

Now what about the mental well-being? When an athlete is preparing for a game, they "get their head in the game." When I'm facing the challenges of the day, running a business, running a household, or just being Mom I often step back and take a breath.

Then I put my desk in order. I prepare for the day, the week, the month. I wrap my head around what must be done.

When I was in college I had to take a speech class. It was the most frightening thing I'd ever done. I was so nervous that I was physically ill every morning. However, I found that if I went in prepared for the class that the fright became controllable. So I would over prepare for the class and practice in front of the mirror. I rehearsed my speech until it rolled off my tongue, easy and routine-like. I had developed a system for overcoming fear.

I use that same technique with my business, my home and my family. I prepare for it. By designing systems to run my business and my home, I have the freedom of mind to enjoy and be there for my family. I took a class many years ago from a man named Paul Dunn. He taught me to "systematize the ordinary things so I can humanize the exceptions." It works! Another great source for systems development is Michael Gerber, author of *The E-Myth.*

For mental and physical fitness, change the daily routine to develop habits to keep you healthy and happy. What are your daily routines? Take note of what you do every day. Do your routines work for you or against you? Do they fit with the *7F Words*™ ?

PANACHE

Cathy

Doing the things we need to do to stay physically and mentally fit and healthy can be challenging. Everyday life seems to get in our way. We get distracted and neglect our own bodies. However, if we can keep the notion of physical and mental health in the forefront of our minds on a daily basis we will be much more apt to practice good habits and achieve our health goals.

The word panache is defined as dash or flamboyance in style and action or a decorative plume of feathers. Notice that it's a seven letter word. My, do we love the number seven. Put a little panache into your fitness routine and think about these seven elements as feathers in your plume.

> **P**lan
> **A**void Excess
> **N**utrients
> **A**ctivities
> **C**alories
> **H**2O
> **E**xercise

Plan

The United States Department of Agriculture, better known as the USDA, has provided a wonderful website that is a treasure trove of information on food and fitness. Visit the website at www.ChooseMyPlate.gov where you can find information on eating right, planning meals, nutrition, and setting and monitoring health goals.

Schedule your daily exercise. Put it on your calendar just as you would any other important event. Why not give yourself the gift of prevention every year and schedule regular checkups with your doctor, dermatologist, dentist and eye doctor during your birthday month? And, while you're still in the office, schedule your next appointment, even if it's for next year. Schedule a vacation, a weekend away or just an hour of "me-time." Everyone needs and deserves time off to rejuvenate.

Getting into the habit of planning your meals can have a significant impact on how well you eat. When you take the time to think about what you're going to eat, you're more likely to make better choices. If you pack a healthy lunch or snack, then you're less likely to stop for that greasy fast food burger or fat-laden fried chicken sandwich. If you don't have to go out at lunch time in search of a meal, you might even find enough time to take a midday walk and enjoy the outdoors.

Avoid Excess

Plainly put, too much sun, alcohol, sodium, nicotine, harsh chemicals, stress and negative influences can drastically reduce your life span. Be kind to your body and mind by limiting your exposure to these things.

I'd like to share my own experience of excess. I was a salt junky for most of my life. Ever since I was a child I would prefer a salty snack to something sweet. I would even go so far as to put salt on an apple. People would tell me to watch the salt because it could cause high blood pressure. Well, my blood pressure was always in the low to normal range and still is, so I thought I had nothing to worry about. Then a few years ago I began to have vicious attacks of vertigo. All of a sudden the world appeared to be spinning out of control. The symptoms were similar to being seasick. At first the attacks would happen only occasionally and then eventually as many as four or five times a week. After almost a year of trying to figure out what was wrong with me, I was diagnosed with Meniere's disease.

Meniere's is a condition that affects the inner ear. The symptoms include vertigo, which is an attack of a dizzy, spinning sensation that causes nausea and vomiting. It also causes hearing loss, tinnitus which is a buzzing or ringing sound in the ear and a sensation of fullness in the ear like when you're at a high altitude and your ear seems clogged. There is no cure for this condition but one of the treatments for Meniere's is a low sodium/salt diet. After being diagnosed I became much more aware and very appalled by the amount of sodium that is contained in the foods we eat every day. Sodium is used as a filler, taste enhancer or preservative in just about every processed food product.

The USDA recommends that most people under age 51 limit their sodium intake to 2300 mg a day. If you're over the age of 51, hypertensive, diabetic or have kidney disease, they recommend a diet that includes not more than 1500 mg of sodium daily. A Crispy Chicken Club Sandwich has 1410 mg of sodium. A Pretzel Salt Bagel without anything on it has 3380 mg of sodium! Have that with an extra-large cappuccino and you add another 480 mg of sodium. Just that meal alone has 3860 mg of sodium, which is almost 168% of the recommended daily allowance for most people.

I try very hard to limit my sodium intake to 1500 mg a day. I must admit there are times when that's very difficult to do; especially around the holidays with all the tempting dishes that grace our table. I am more motivated to limit my sodium intake than most people I know because too much sodium can lead to very serious consequences for me. As a result of too much sodium I've lost about 80% of the hearing in my left ear and have spent many a day in bed praying for the room to stop spinning. So far my right ear has not been affected by Meniere's disease and I plan to keep it that way by limiting my sodium intake and making sure that I have the nutrients I need every day to keep my body healthy.

When you begin to monitor your sodium intake you will be shocked at how much you're actually consuming on a daily basis. Salt is lurking everywhere, even in foods that taste more sweet than salty, like breads, cakes and cookies.

Nutrients

Everyone needs adequate vitamins, minerals, protein, calcium, fiber, anti-oxidants and other nutrients daily to maintain good physical and mental health and to prevent disease. We are not trained medical professionals or nutritionists so we cannot advise you on what specifically you will need for your optimal health. We highly recommend that you consult with your medical professional for the right plan to meet your individual needs.

At www.ChooseMyPlate.gov you can sign up for the SuperTracker. There you can look up the nutritional information on over 8,000 foods. You can also use the plan which shows your daily food group targets – what and how much to eat based on your nutrient needs and your personal calorie goal. When you plan your meals take your nutritional needs into account. That way you will get the important nutrients you need and you'll be better able to control your portion sizes.

Activities

We have resolved to live our lives with purpose and intent. One of the reasons we wrote this book is to help others do the same. We make choices every day about the activities in which we engage. Sometimes those choices are made with little conscious effort, simply by reacting to situations throughout the day. To make the most of our day we need to make the majority of our activities those that we consciously choose to do.

In our Daily Oath we pledge to, "Allow myself the Freedom to say no to things I do not want to do or that will not advance me toward my goals." In that oath we also pledge to focus, have faith in ourselves, nurture our relationships, act in ways that enhance our financial situation, take action to ensure mental and physical fitness and to have fun. You might ask, with a limited amount of time in every day, how you can possibly do all that? The answer is choosing your activities wisely and making a conscious effort to make every moment count.

One way to get the most out of the day is to combine activities to cover multiple elements of the *7F Words*™. I combine Fitness, Fun and Family by taking ballroom dance lessons with my husband. Deborah and her husband work together in their real estate business so they are combining Family with Finance. Barbara combines Fitness with Fun during her morning workouts. She combines Freedom with Finance by teaching her clients how to become debt free. I enjoy playing Words With Friends™ on Facebook. I love that game and I play it with friends and family who are not local. That way I connect with people who are important to me and I have fun at the same time.

Whether you're engaged in an activity that you planned or you're simply doing something in response to a situation, by stepping back and asking yourself, "Will doing this advance me toward my goals?" will help you judge whether the activity is worth it or not. Engaging in and completing activities that give you a sense of purpose, fulfillment or accomplishment or that bring you joy and happiness go a long way to improving your mental fitness. Ruthlessly prioritize your activities to maximize the good things and eliminate the things that bring you down.

Calories

Calories are a measurement tool, like inches or ounces. They measure the energy a food or beverage provides from the carbohydrate, fat, protein and alcohol it contains. Calories are the fuel we need to work and play. We even need calories to rest and sleep. Foods and beverages vary in how many calories and nutrients they contain. When choosing what to eat and drink, it's important to get the right mix - enough nutrients, but not too many calories.

Eating a cookie that has 100 calories will not give us the same nutritional benefits as eating 100 calories worth of lean meat or spinach. Eating the cookie is okay once we've rewarded our bodies with the quality foods that are loaded with nourishing protein, fiber, vitamins and minerals.

According to the USDA, women between the ages of 31 to 50 who are not physically active require 1800 calories daily, while men in that age group require 2200 calories. Your personal daily calorie limit depends on your age, sex, height, weight, and activity level. Visit www.ChooseMyPlate.gov where you can find specific information. If you want to maintain a healthy weight you must be aware of how many calories you consume and stay within the daily recommended number for your age, height, weight, and activity level.

H2O

Drinking an adequate amount of water is essential to good health. However, the big question is what is an adequate amount of water? In an article by the Mayo Clinic staff they explain that there is no simple answer to that question. They state that studies have produced varying recommendations. The amount of water you need depends on several factors including your health, how active you are and the climate you live in. Water is necessary for keeping our organs running smoothly. It flushes out toxins, carries nutrients to our cells and provides moisture to our ears, nose and throat. Dehydration, which is basically an insufficient amount of water in your body, can drain your energy, make you tired, cause headaches and eventually lead to death.

The Institute of Medicine determined that an adequate intake (AI) for a healthy male living in a temperate climate is about 13 cups of total beverages a day. The AI for women is about 9 cups of total beverages a day. The water you drink provides about 80 percent of the total water intake. The other 20 percent comes from the food you eat such as fruits and vegetables, another good reason to eat fresh fruits and vegetables daily. Beverages such as milk, juice, coffee, tea or soda contribute to the AI, but should not be the major portion of your daily total fluid intake. For more information visit: www.mayoclinic.com/health/water/NU00283.

Based on this information, I calculate that I need to drink about 58 ounces of water daily. The standard water bottles that are sold in cases just about everywhere hold about 17 fluid ounces. I figure I need to drink between 3 and 4 bottles a day. For me that's a very tall order, so my target is three bottles. To keep myself on track I devised this little trick. In the morning I start out with a bottle of water. I put three rubber bands on the bottom portion of the bottle. Every time I finish the bottle I move one of the rubber bands to the top and refill the bottle. At the end of the day, if I've met my water intake goal, all of my rubber bands will be at the top portion of the bottle.

Exercise

The National Institute on Aging (NIA) at the National Institute of Health (NIH) lists four types of physical exercise: Endurance or aerobic activities that increase the heart rate and breathing; Strength exercises like weight lifting that increase muscle strength; Balance which helps to prevent falls and Flexibility exercises like Yoga that stretch the muscles. It's recommended that you integrate as many of these styles into your daily routine as possible.

The NIA has introduced *Go4Life®* which is designed to help adults 50 and older incorporate more exercise and physical activity into their daily lives. On the *Go4Life®* website you can watch exercise videos, submit your own exercise success stories, print educational tip sheets and use the interactive tools in the *MyGo4Life®* section to make an exercise plan and track your progress over time. See more at http://go4life.nia.nih.gov.

According to the American Heart Association, "It's most helpful to do moderately intense aerobic physical activity for at least 30 minutes on most or all days of the week. A good guideline: Work hard enough to breathe harder but still be able to carry on a conversation." www.heart.org.

Christine King, founder of *Your Best Fit* in Boynton Beach, FL shared her incredible story with us in one of our internet TV programs. This excerpt is from her website: http://lifeonlybetter.com.

"In July of 1996, she was involved in a serious Jet Ski accident, which left her with a broken back. Six months prior to this terrible accident, she was in vigorous training for the Miss Fitness USA Contest. The accident caused an explosion of a lower lumbar vertebra.

Doctors were unable to say whether Christine would ever walk again. In emergency surgery, bone was taken from her hip to replace what had burst in her back. Two rods and four pins were inserted to hold her back together.

After the surgery, the doctors informed Christine the operation was a success. Although her back had been repaired, they were still unsure of the amount of nerve damage and internal injuries. After a rigorous rehabilitation, doctors were confident that she would regain most of the mobility in her lower extremities. The doctors also told Christine that the superior physical condition she was in prior to the accident is the primary reason she would be able to walk again..."

Christine says that you're never too old to change your body for the better, even if you're 100 years old. She told the story of one of her clients who was close to 100. He came to her because he wanted to improve his tennis game! Christine suggests that to achieve success in an exercise program you need one that works for you. She advises consulting with a professional who can do a proper assessment; and to work with someone who has experience and can design a program that works you slowly. She gave us these valuable tips:

- If it hurts, don't do it
- If it's too heavy, don't lift it
- If you get too tired, stop

• • • • • • •

Power Strategy #6: Put Panache into Your Routine

It's interesting how many excuses we can come up with for not making Fitness a priority: no time, an injury, it's expensive, no motivation, it's not urgent, had to take the dog to the vet, etc. How many reasons can you come up with to make Fitness a *priority* in your life?

Focus on *doing* something that you can reasonably do to get moving. Watch your portions size and the quality of the food you consume. If you want a cookie then eat *a* cookie. Remember the anagram for PANACHE and put some flamboyance into your actions.

Plan

Avoid Excess

Nutrients

Activities

Calories

H2O

Exercise

How many feathers can you put into your plume each day?

This book is not designed to nor does it provide medical advice. You should not use any of the information in place of a visit or consultation with your physician or other healthcare provider.

"Baseball is ninety percent mental and the other half is physical."
Yogi Berra

"You are today what your choices were yesterday, you will be tomorrow what your choices are today."
Sheena Temple

And, last but not least, today I will have
<u>Fun</u>.

Fun: delight, distraction, diversion, entertainment, pleasure, recreation

Chapter 7

Fun

"Work should be nothing more than productive play."
Dr. Robert Porte

Enjoy the Journey

Cathy

Before we began writing this book I sometimes found myself feeling a sense of guilt if I was having fun. In my mind, having a good time somehow equated to a lack of productivity. After all, how could I be working toward my goals if I was having fun? Now one of my goals is to put some fun into everything I do.

Fun can be woven into just about every aspect of our lives. Each of the other six "F" words provides us with unlimited opportunities to have fun and enjoy a positive and balanced life.

In the chapter on Focus we talked about setting a goal to do something fun. Not only can the outcome of the goal be enjoyable but the exercise in goal-setting itself can also be a fun activity, especially when you're doing it with someone you care about.

During the summer of 2012 Jim and I took a long-wished-for trip to Italy. We invited my cousin Tony and his wife Janet to join us. Tony and I planned most of the 20-day trip. We spent ten days on a structured tour of Sicily and during the remaining ten days we traveled to Sorrento, Rome, Florence and Venice.

Tony and Janet live in Savannah, Georgia while Jim and I are in Delray Beach, Florida, so the planning had to be done via phone and e-mail. We each bought a copy of *Rick Steves'* travel guide. Throughout our planning we would read about a city then call each other to discuss which points of interest we wanted to see. We went on the internet to find the best deals on hotels, planes, trains and buses. Tony would find great travel items in stores and take a picture with his iPhone and text it to me. We had a fabulous time on the trip, and planning the trip was also tons of fun. It was a wonderful bonding experience for us cousins who don't get to see each other very often.

Our trip to Italy was expensive and well worth every penny. However, fun doesn't have to be expensive. As a matter of fact some of the most enjoyable things I've done have cost next to nothing.

Seven Under Seven

Cathy

Here are seven FUN ideas that a family of four can do for under $7. Notice that they all start with F.

1. Farkle™– The word itself tends to make you laugh. It sounds a little naughty but everyone loves to yell it once the game gets going. This is a really fun game that my family and I play at most family get-togethers, especially during our annual family reunion at our timeshare on the Gulf Coast of Florida.

   Imagine your family sitting around your kitchen or dining room table on a Saturday night. Everyone has their favorite drink in hand. You pull out six dice, a pencil and pad of paper. The first player rolls the six dice and they roll at least a five or a one. Then they roll again, they get at least another one or a five, they roll again, and oops, no one or five, everyone yells FARKLE! This sounds a little simple, but it's actually a risk-taking game that requires some decision-making, a bit of strategy and a lot of luck. Do you take a risk and keep rolling to increase your score or do you ignore the other players chanting, "Roll, roll" to play it safe and stop while you're ahead?

   The object of the game is to be the first to get 10,000 points. It's a fight to the finish that tends to get a little rowdy at times. The game is designed for two or more players, but definitely the more the merrier, as long as you don't have too many to record the scores. My husband likes to keep score on an Excel™ spreadsheet. He breaks out his laptop whenever we decide to play. The game is recommended for players eight years or older, but we include the younger ones as well. As long as they don't swallow the dice they'll have a blast, too.

You can find a Complete Farkle™ Instruction Video at www.OhFarkle.com or buy the Farkle™ Game by Patch Products at your local Target or Wal-Mart for less than $5.00. The six dice come in a sturdy plastic cup for shaking and throwing. When you're finished playing, just throw the dice in along with the instructions, snap on the lid and store for the next fun event.

2. Frisbee™ – According to Wikipedia this flying disc got its beginning in 1938 when Fred Morrison and his wife Lucille were offered 25 cents for a cake pan that they were tossing back and forth to each other on a beach in Santa Monica, California. Since they had only paid 5 cents for the cake pan they saw a great business opportunity in flying discs.

The Frisbee™, a product of Wham-O, has evolved quite a bit since the flying cake pan, but you can still buy one for well under $7.00. A couple of hours at the park, beach or your own back yard can provide a ton of family fun and great exercise, too. You can even include your dog in this activity, but be sure to get a Frisbee™ that is made for dogs. These are slower flying discs made of more pliable material to prevent injury to your pet.

3. Fly a Kite – I remember the sense of exhilaration I would get as a child when I would fly a kite in the middle of our street. I would make my kites out of newspaper, string and old cloth; and they flew really well. I recently saw my neighbor and her little girl flying a kite in the middle of my street. It brought back great memories. I was chomping at the bit to get into the action so I went to Wal-Mart and picked one up for $1.37. Making your own though can be a lot more fun. Here are a few websites about kites and how to make your own.

https://en.wikipedia.org/wiki/Kite

http://kite.org/
http://www.wikihow.com/Make-a-Fast-Kite-with-One-Sheet-of-Paper

4. Foxtrot – The Foxtrot is a beautiful ballroom dance that can be enjoyed by just about anyone who can walk. Ballroom dancing has become more and more popular in recent years. TV shows like *Dancing with the Stars, So You Think You Can Dance* and *America's Got Talent* all showcase elegant ballroom dancing.

Jim and I recently began taking ballroom dance lessons from a very talented dance instructor who is now in his 80's. The fun and physical activity of dance has kept the dance instructor young and fit. The basic Foxtrot steps which are forward and backward walking and side steps are fairly easy to master. Numerous videos on this subject can be found on www.YouTube.com. The Quick Beginners Foxtrot lesson by Teresa Mason teaches the basic dance steps in an easy to grasp manner that can get anyone going quickly. At the time of this writing this YouTube video had almost 700,000 views! Or you can watch Dance Instructor Terry Dean demonstrate the Foxtrot on MonkeySee.com.
http://www.monkeysee.com/video_clips/1392-ballroom-dancing-how-to-foxtrot

So, plan a night with your loved ones. Move the furniture out of the way, pull up an instructional video on the web, put on some music and learn to dance the Foxtrot.

Remember to have fun with this and don't take yourself too seriously. Giggle when you trip over each other's feet or totally forget the steps. And, as they say, "dance like no one's watching."

5. Finger Painting – Remember how much fun you had finger painting as a child mixing the colors, feeling the paint ooze through your fingers and creating a great design or picture of your very own? Well, why not share that fun all over again with the people you love? Young or old, anyone can benefit from the joys of getting creative with paint. Simple finger painting can be done on almost any medium you have around the house; paper bags, cardboard, poster board, or construction paper. You can buy a set of finger paints for under $5.00 or you can make your own using sugar, salt, corn starch, water and food coloring. You can find the recipe at:

http://lifeasmom.com/2013/05/homemade-finger-paint.html

Get inspired by the season and create holiday decorations or gift wrapping. Wouldn't it be fun to go out into nature with the family and find an inspirational piece, like a shell, a piece of driftwood or perhaps a beautiful flower or leaf to include in your masterpiece?

6. Fashion Night – Pull out some old jeans and/or tee-shirts. Go on a scavenger hunt around the house and gather things like old buttons, glitter, fabric scraps, shells, old jewelry, etc. Guys, go into your tool box and pull out some nuts and bolts, washers, bits of wire, etc. Then everyone have fun decorating their individual garments. See who can come up with the most creative design.

7. Film Night – Look for inexpensive DVD rentals in your community. Or, go to your local library and pick out one or two movies. In South Florida you can rent a DVD movie for $1.00 at the local grocery store. Select a movie that the whole family will enjoy. If you don't have a DVD player then plan in advance by looking up the TV schedule. Buy a large bag of popcorn and a bottle of your favorite beverage or better yet, pop your own and make some flavored iced tea or hot chocolate depending on the season.

   Or, if you really want to get creative make your own little film using your camcorder or smart phone and post it on YouTube for everyone to enjoy.

These are 7 ideas that begin with the letter F. Imagine how many ideas you could come up with if you used every letter in the alphabet!

Find the Fun, Forget the Stress

Deborah

My customer, Dr. Lee, has a wonderful outlook on life and packs as much fun into each day as possible. Instead of a simple "Hello" he likes to greet people with "Happy Birthday!" He believes you should treat every day like it's your birthday. I love getting emails from Dr. Lee because the subject line to me always reads "Happy Birthday!" Wouldn't it be wonderful to have a little birthday celebration every day?

A key to having fun is to train your mind to look for opportunities everywhere. Try to find the positive or the humor in every situation. Putting yourself into the right frame of mind before beginning anything can make the difference between the situation becoming a delight or a chore.

Every year at the Women's Council of REALTORS® Installation Banquet, the Past Presidents line up on stage and pass the gavel from the previous years Past Presidents to the newest. One year we forgot to bring the gavel. After a frenzied discussion someone with a great sense of humor went to the kitchen and found a meat mallet. So we passed the meat mallet from Past President to Past President right on up to the new President. We all laughed the whole time. We took what could have been a disaster and turned it into to something fun.

Fun can happen anywhere and at any time, whether it is at an office meeting or baking cookies with your family. What are you doing to find the fun and forget the stress?

Productive Play

Cathy

Work is not an "F" word, but it certainly plays a major role in most of our lives. Many years ago a good friend told me that, "Work should be nothing more than productive play." This thought or philosophy has stayed with me through my various careers. Every job has its good and not-so-good aspects. However, the key to having fun in your job is to find something to do that you're passionate about. If you focus on the elements of your job that bring you pleasure and try to amplify them it's a great deal easier to tolerate the things that are less enjoyable or challenge you.

Can you think of some ways to make work more fun? Fun might be impromptu celebrations like King Cake on Fat Tuesday. Or it might be to invite the office next door over for coffee, take a friend to lunch, have birthday cupcakes, or bring flowers from your garden to a coworker. One of Barbara's clients hangs $5 bills on the bulletin board. Every time one of the technicians sells a service contract they get to put their name on the board and take a $5 bill. It's fun to see who can collect the most money. A little creativity goes a long way to making work more fun.

Is it F2 or F3?

Barbara

When it comes to family vacations do you categorize them as F2 "Family Fun" or F3 "Forced Family Fun"? Dave and I take our children and ride the Amtrak from California to Texas every year to visit family. We spend two nights on the train in our private sleeper compartments. The four of us enjoy our meals in the dining car complete with white tablecloths. Dave and I have a cocktail in the observation car while we enjoy watching the landscape go by. We can see rivers and canyons, rolling hills and bridges. We can even see into Mexico as we travel through El Paso. Our children enjoy going to the snack car and playing cards or watching a movie together on the iPad. My friend Jennifer called me the first time we took the train and she asked me, "Was it an F2 or F3?" For Dave and me these trips are usually F2. Our children tease that they are F3, but I know they will have fond memories of these train trips to Texas every year.

· · · · · · ·

Power Strategy #7: Enjoy the Journey

Make every day a 7, and intentionally build fun into every aspect of your life. Enjoy the journey not just the destination by purposefully living in the moment. Transform work into productive play by amplifying the good parts. Fun doesn't have to be expensive; the good things in life are free. Reduce your stress by being willing to laugh at yourself.

What is your version of Fun?

How can you make work nothing more than productive play?

What have you done in the past that was fun?

How can you recreate that moment and be intentional about having fun today?

"People rarely succeed unless they have fun in what they are doing."
Dale Carnegie

"It's kind of fun to do the impossible."
Walt Disney

"Today was good. Today was fun. Tomorrow is another one."
Dr. Seuss

"Success is not the key to happiness. Happiness is the key to success. If you love what you are doing, you will be successful."
Albert Schweitzer

Transformation Stories

The *7F Words*™ Journey and How I've Changed

Barbara's Story

Five years ago I took a leap of faith and started a tax planning and preparation business in a town of 25,000 people. I had no connections, no influential acquaintances, no friends and no immediate family anywhere near. I could have crawled back into my comfortable space, picked up a good book to read and I would have been happy for a while. But I knew that would not satisfy me for long.

I looked around and saw an opportunity. With only two other CPAs in public practice I thought there was plenty of work to go around. So I rented a space, bought some really cheap office furniture and interviewed my first hire while screwing chairs together. We sat on the empty boxes while we chatted. So now I had an employee. Wow!

It came time to open for business. With nervous anticipation we unlocked the door and waited. Tick-tock, tick-tock went the clock. I had faith that the first customer would come. And he did! Jack walked through the door and said "Barbara, I'm so glad you're here. We met a few months ago and I'm looking forward to working with you."

It was music to my ears. That first year I picked up over 100 new customers and we've grown every year, thanks in part to our many customers who have referred others to us.

Now I was not only serving my customers, staying at the office until midnight preparing tax returns, I was then staying up until midnight the next day paying the bills, then going home and collapsing with a glass of wine. I had created a new business, but it was a nightmare. I was doing everything from opening the door in the morning and answering the phone, to meeting with clients, shopping for supplies and cleaning the bathroom. Then I still had to be a good mother, going to flag football practice, helping with homework, cooking a healthy dinner and paying some attention to my loving husband. I was doing EVERYTHING. Boy, I had it all and then some. Yikes!

This was about the time I turned 50. I was determined that I would be "50 and fabulous." I did not like how I was beginning to sag in places that were "never to be seen" and I had this overall feeling of sluggishness. So I hired a personal trainer and told my team at the office that I would be in late on Tuesdays and Thursdays.

I was working on the business systems to make the day-to-day operation run a little smoother. My employees needed training to enable them to be the best at their jobs; they grew exponentially in a very short time. It set the stage so I could be free from the business and do other things. I was beginning to see a bigger picture. I realized my time was my most valuable and limited asset.

If I was going to fit in all the things that were important to me, I would have to make a plan and block time for it. This meant that I had to let go of a few things. So I did what I always do, I made a list. I wrote down everything I do in a typical day. Then I wrote a name next to each item on the list. This was my delegation list. I gave the household chores to my two sons. Since they would have to fend for themselves someday, they needed to know how to do a few things like cooking, cleaning and laundry. We had a few interesting mishaps ... but it all worked out just fine.

There were tasks on the list that my employees could easily take on, like answering the phone, going to the post office and ordering supplies. I cut back on checking email and Facebook every three minutes to once a day. I set aside specific blocks of time to return phone calls. I set aside certain days to take client appointments. I made some very important changes that freed up my time to pursue my other goals such as writing a book.

Then Deborah and Cathy approached me with the *7F Words™* book idea and asked if I would contribute to the Finance section. I jumped at the chance. And the roller coaster ride began.

I revisited my "list" and realized the important items left on the list that I had not delegated to someone else included the *7F Words™*.

I had written the following:

- Focus on my Family while my boys are still young enough to be influenced by my presence.
- Embrace Faith in my own abilities and continue my relationship with God. Start every day with gratitude for my life, a heavenly cup of coffee, a warm bed and my loving family.
- Freedom to say "no" without guilt to the things that don't fit my plan. Ruthlessly prioritize my time.
- Work on my Finances and finally have my credit cards paid off. Put money in savings every month.
- Fitness program twice a week with my trainer. (My overall strength is amazing. I'm lifting twice as much weight and my body fat ratio is down to low/normal.)
- Take time to have Fun such as long drives visiting places I want to see, sitting by my pool with friends, a book club, romantic evenings with my husband, and enjoyable dinners with my entire family.

Putting my Focus on Faith, Freedom, Family, Finance, Fitness and Fun ensures that my life is balanced. With planning and focus the important stuff does not take a back seat. The *7F Words*™ is the key to living life on purpose and with intent. Now I'm in control. I'm in the driver's seat, enjoying the ride!

Having the Time of My Life

Cathy's Story

These days when someone asks me how I'm doing, I can honestly reply, "I am having the time of my life." The *7F Words*™ have brought me to this marvelous place. More than ever before, I'm living my life with purpose and intent. Each and every day, I try to deliberately touch on every one of the seven elements, even if it's only in a very small way.

Several years ago I was in a very dark place. My world was falling apart from the symptoms I was experiencing from Meniere's disease. For a couple of years Meniere's wreaked havoc with my inner ear and caused me to have severe episodes of vertigo, as often as four or five times a week. Sometimes when I lay in bed, not able to keep any food down and trying to get the room to stop spinning, I would think I would be better off not living. Now, don't get me wrong, I would never consider taking my own life, but if it just happened to turn out that way, I felt like it would be okay with me. I persevered through the symptoms, but in the end I had to make a conscious decision to sacrifice the hearing in my left ear in order to get my life back. If anyone had told me back then what my life would be like now I would not have believed them. Today I'm enjoying my life to the fullest.

I keep the *7F Words*™ Daily Oath posted above my desk and I also carry it in my purse. I recite it often to remind myself to focus on the important things.

I am so much more grateful for what I have and the joy and peace that is bestowed on me every day. I've gained a much better appreciation for the little things in life, that don't have material value and I put much less emphasis in accumulating things. My life is much less cluttered.

I've developed a heightened sense of what brings me pleasure and fulfillment. I concentrate on those things and let go of the things that cause me stress. I've even learned to say no without feeling guilty or fear of not being liked or appreciated.

I make a conscious effort to spend more quality time with my family and truly value the wonderful relationships I've developed with the people who have significance in my life.

Through my experiences with Meniere's disease and the research I've done for this book, I no longer take my health for granted. Although I am nowhere close to being in perfect condition, I do strive to eat better and exercise more.

Fun has become an important element in my life. I find I'm much more productive when I'm having fun. I look for the humor in challenging situations and laugh at myself a lot.

I'm aware that down the road I will encounter adversity and sorrow; everyone does. At that point in time I am sure I won't feel like I'm having the time of my life. I know that if I focus on the good, have faith and keep seeking balance I will surely come through to a better day.

It's often said that "Two heads are better than one." I've learned that three heads are much better than one. Deborah, Barbara and I have produced something much bigger than any one of us could have on our own. From this synergy, I have gained more confidence in my own ability and our joint ability to accomplish whatever it is we set out to do with this book and the larger endeavor of Certified Sisters, Inc. I hope we have inspired you to live your life with joy and purpose, starting with today.

Divine Direction

Deborah's Story

Many years ago one of my favorite customers gave me a book by Trina Paulus called *Hope for the Flowers*. The book tells the story of two caterpillars, Stripe and Yellow and their struggle to climb to the top of their caterpillar pile. As they climbed they gradually realized that getting to the top was not as wonderful as others portrayed it to be. They learned that the caterpillars that got out of the race to the top were able to stop for a while and break free of their past. After a period of cocooning they became the beautiful butterflies they were meant to be.

As I think back I realize that, at one time, I was just like Stripe and Yellow. I was in the race to the top. For many years, my husband and I worked feverishly to build our real estate business. We were successful. We sacrificed a lot, but we also reaped many benefits. Then Hurricane Wilma took off the back half of our office condo. While we were busy rebuilding our lives and our office, the financial tsunami hit and the bottom fell out of the real estate market.

Throughout my life, no matter what challenges I faced, I would just pick myself up, brush myself off, and move forward on my trek to the top. Taking that approach, I just kept moving along working harder and harder earning less and less money. Through this struggle I neglected my family and my friends. I kept telling myself that everything would be okay once the next real estate deal closed.

Like many small real estate brokerages during that time, we were not bringing in enough money to cover our expenses. But, pride would not allow us to give up. So, we mortgaged everything we could, sold my jewelry and continued to hold on for dear life. At one point our financial situation became so bad that we had to swallow our pride and accept help from our friends, family and our church.

A friend from my prayer group invited me to join a professional networking organization that was just starting up. At that time, the membership fee seemed expensive, but I took a leap of faith and joined. A few months later, because of connections in that networking group, I was offered a job managing a new real estate office. It was just the financial cushion we needed. I accepted the position.

When some people hit bottom they either blame God or turn away from God. When I hit bottom I turned to God. I don't know where I would have ended up, if I had not had my faith to give me hope in a brighter future.

After a couple of years of building that real estate business the owners decided to divest of certain assets and sold the business to another brokerage. I was devastated. I had poured my heart and soul into building the business, as if it were my own. I felt as though a door had slammed in my face and I prayed for direction.

When I was at the Florida REALTORS® Convention, my hotel room was between two banks of elevators. I could've gone either left or right to reach the elevators. I chose to go right. As the elevator doors began to close I saw someone coming down the hall, so I held the door for him. It turned out he was someone I was told to meet who might be able to help with my career. I made arrangements to meet with him again and left feeling certain that the encounter was one of God's endeavors to put me in the right place at the right time.

When I returned from the convention, I shared my story with my Bible study group. I told them that I believed it was God showing me he was answering my prayers, as I always prayed for Him to direct my steps and guide me either to the right or to the left. They started laughing at me. When I asked why they were laughing, they told me to turn around and look at the classroom bulletin board. On it was this verse, "Whether you turn to the right or to the left, your ears will hear a voice behind you, saying this is the way, walk in it." Isaiah 30:21.

I look back at that situation now and realize that presenting me with another career challenge was just God's way of getting me to take another path. Today, thanks to all my great customers who continue to support me, we have a new and thriving real estate business. We also have the Certified Sisters, Inc., the *7F Words*™ book, personal coaching and workshops.

I'm committed to avoiding the mistakes of the past. I've learned to balance work with the other more important elements of life. The *7F Words*™ journey has really opened my eyes. My faith in God continues to grow. My focus is much more intent. My family is of the utmost importance to me. My physical fitness, which was neglected for so long while I was struggling, has become a top priority. The freedom to be my own boss is a wonderful gift that

I will never give away again. I'm still working on my finances. My goal is to become debt free and remain that way. And, last but not least I am trying to incorporate fun into everything I do. Life is too short not to enjoy every day.

I greatly appreciate all the people who were there to help me, when I needed help the most. My goal is to pay it forward and help others as well.

Whatever is happening in your life, I encourage you to let go and let the wind blow you where God wants you to be. I hope that by implementing the ideas from the *7F Words™* you too can stop, cocoon for a while, then break free of the past and become all that you are meant to be. Thank you for allowing us to share the *7F Words™* and what the journey has meant to us. May God bless you on your journey.

About the Authors

Barbara D. Agerton is a Certified Public Accountant. She is originally from Louisville, Kentucky. She received a BBA in Accounting from the University of Texas at Arlington. After completing the CPA exam she went on to obtain a Master of Accountancy from the University of West Florida. As a Federal and State Tax Manager with KPMG Peat Marwick she increased her knowledge of tax law for individuals and small business owners. She now owns Agerton Enterprises, Inc. and loves to help her clients with their tax and business needs. Barbara is an educator at heart and teaches others how to take control of their finances. Barbara lives in Ridgecrest, California with her husband and two sons.

Deborah A. Bacarella is the Real Estate Broker/Owner of Elite Florida Real Estate in Boca Raton, Florida. With over 33 years of experience, she enjoys helping buyers navigate the way to their dream home. Deborah is a dedicated professional with a talent for putting buyers and sellers together. The awards from her peers and testimonials from her customers attest to her outstanding results. Deborah is a Certified Professional Coach and Real Estate Instructor. Deborah loves life in Florida with her husband and three amazing children.

Catherine A. Lewis (Cathy) is a practicing Realtor® in Palm Beach County, Florida. As a Certified Professional Coach and Realtor® Cathy fulfills her passion for helping people by assisting them in finding their "Slice of Paradise". She is originally from Staten Island, New York. Cathy earned a B.S. in Business Administration from Nova Southeastern University and holds several designations from the National Association of Realtors. Prior to going into real estate, Cathy was a corporate trainer who focused on teaching supervisory and management skills at two Fortune 500 companies. Cathy lives in Delray Beach, Florida with her husband and two sons.

References

Some of our favorite resources for living a balanced life.

www.empower-yourself-with-color-psychology.com The inspiration for our colors.

www.luannslensphotography.com LuAnn Warner-Prokos for awesome photography

www.ccstampworks.com Harry L. Chester for the eagle print in the Freedom chapter.

www.revolverlouisville.com Tom Gnadinger Photography for the family photo.

www.pelproductions.com Patrick E. Lewis videographer

art4brian@bellsouth.net Brian Rothschild, owner of GraphicFXOnline Studios for graphics and layout.

Focus

www.evernote.com to capture and save online info that you want to reference later. You can see your Evernote files online from anywhere you have an internet connection.

www.lynda.com for video training on how to do lots of stuff. Mostly how to use computer programs such as office, adobe creative suite but also to learn how to use your digital camera.

www.dropbox.com or http://drive.google.com for storing and sharing documents and photos. Use these to collaborate on a project. It makes it so easy to share.

Faith

www.tonyrobbins.com for motivation and encouragement

http://www.oprah.com/oprahs-lifeclass/oprahs-lifeclass.html is full of helpful advice

www.vitalaffirmations.com is a good source for affirmations for various life circumstances

www.momsinprayer.org Moms In Prayer

www.bsfinternational.org Bible Study Fellowship International

Freedom

www.dalemannodesigns.com for ideas to organize your space.

www.entrepreneur.com for great articles on time management.

Family

www.skype.com for keeping up with far away friends and family.

www.apple.com FaceTime for the iPhone or iPad is also a great way to video chat with friends and family. Use it to video call clients all over the world.

http://www.viber.com/ Free calls, text and picture sharing with anyone, anywhere.

Finances

www.daveramsey.com for great info on getting out of debt.

www.kiplingers.com for the latest financial and tax related news.

www.emyth.com and the book *The E-myth Revisited* by Michael Gerber. These are a must have for any new business owner or if you are thinking of starting a business.

www.carbonite.com is an easy to use online backup.

www.etsy.com to sell your craft projects

www.elance.com to sell your freelance services

Fitness

www.myfitnesspal.com for tracking meals and workouts each day. It has a reference library for nutritional content of many brand name foods. It's very handy when you are eating out.

www.beachbody.com P90X web app for iPad. Take your workout anywhere.

www.beyonddiet.com by Isabel De Los Rios is a great source for diet and nutrition information. Her readers supply new recipes all the time. Isabel inspires me to cook healthy meals.

www.mayoclinic.com/health/water/NU00283 for info on water recommendations.

www.ChooseMyPlate.gov for information on eating right, planning meals, nutrition, and setting and monitoring health goals

www.annieappleseedproject.org provides information, education, advocacy, and awareness for people with cancer, their family and friends.

Fun

www.shutterfly.com for sharing photos, create photo gifts such as calendars and photo books and photo cards.

www.facebook.com for seeing what all your friends are up to.

www.travelocity.com for finding great prices on air, hotel and car travel.

www.vrbo.com Privately owned properties all over the world available for your family vacation.

www.OhFarkle.com Complete Farkle™ Instruction Video

http://lifeasmom.com/2013/05/homemade-finger-paint.html Finger paint recipe.

http://www.monkeysee.com/video_clips/ Dance Instructor, Terry Dean demonstrates the Foxtrot

https://en.wikipedia.org/wiki/Kite;

http://kite.org/;

http://www.wikihow.com/Make-a-Fast-Kite-with-One-Sheet-of-Paper Websites about kites and how to make your own.

To bring a life-changing *7F Words*™ workshop to your association, group or club, or to order additional copies of the book

7F Words™ *For Living a Balanced Life*

Power Strategies to Transform Your Life

Email: info@7FWords.com

Call: 1-707-7FWords

Visit: www.7FWords.com

We'd love to hear what you have done to create more balance in your life. Share your story with us at www.7FWords.com.

Notes

Made in the USA
Charleston, SC
03 November 2014